LIVING A BALANCED LIFE...

BODY, MIND AND SPIRIT

CHUCK SALISBURY

New York

LIVING A BALANCED LIFE...
BODY, MIND AND SPIRIT

CHUCK SALISBURY

ISBN 978-1-61448-008-2 PB
ISBN 978-1-61448-009-9 EB (paperback)

Library of Congress Control Number: 2011927223

Published by:
Morgan James Publishing
The Entrepreneurial Publisher
5 Penn Plaza, 23rd Floor
New York City, New York 10001
(212) 655-5470 Office
(516) 908-4496 Fax
www.MorganJamesPublishing.com

Cover Design by:
Rachel Lopez
rachel@r2cdesign.com

Interior Design by:
Bonnie Bushman
bbushman@bresnan.net

In an effort to support local communities, raise awareness and funds, Morgan James Publishing donates one percent of all book sales for the life of each book to Habitat for Humanity.
Get involved today, visit
www.HelpHabitatForHumanity.org.

SERMONS

By Edgar A. Guest

I'd rather see a sermon than hear one any day,
I'd rather one should walk with me than merely show the way.

The eye's a better pupil and more willing than the ear;
Fine counsel is confusing, but example's always clear;

And the best of all the preachers are the men who live their creeds,
For to see the good in action is what everybody needs.

I can soon learn how to do it if you'll let me see it done.
I can watch your hands in action, but your tongue too fast may run.

And the lectures your deliver may be very wise and true;
But I'd rather get my lesson by observing what you do.

For I may misunderstand you and the high advice you give,
But there's no misunderstanding how you act and how you live.

CONTENTS

Introduction

"It is Finished."

These are the final words uttered by Jesus Christ as he died on the Cross. They were an acknowledgement that His body was failing as His time on earth as a living representative of God was over. Those who viewed his death must have felt an overwhelming sense of bewilderment—His followers had come to accept Him as the Son of God, not just a mortal man. They believed that He was immortal, and that he could triumph over any mortal man including Herod and the Pharisees. They saw him raise the dead, heal the sick and restore sight to the blind. This belief in Jesus remained strong until those fateful words were uttered. But as His body died and the belief in Jesus as an immortal *earthly* being faded away, He gave life to an even stronger conviction in the truth of His words. The resurrection was a new beginning that confirmed, for the first time, that His ministry was 100% truthful. Promises of eternal life were now validated, and Jesus indeed emerged triumphant over mortal men.

It may seem strange to begin a book with the words Jesus used to close the chapter of His life on earth. But these words aren't just an ending. They are an invitation to us to appreciate the grace of new beginnings awarded through our faith, to marvel at the power of God and the love He has for us. This book is written in the spirit of that invitation. I want to show you how you, too, can use the gifts given to you by God to close one chapter of your life and begin a new one—healthier, happier and stronger in your faith than ever.

This is a faith-based book and uses the Bible as its main source of reference. We see from innumerable examples in the Bible that living a balanced life requires us to pay attention to our bodies, our minds and our spirits, all at once. We must take care of God's temple—our bodies—and use the untapped resources of our mind. Once we learn to take care of ourselves, we can recognize that we constantly receive ideas and signs from our Creator. He is the "spirit" within us, driving us in our day-to-day lives to succeed, be happy and fulfill His mission for each of us. If we don't use the gifts God has given us, we'll lose them—and if we don't react to the signs He sends us, we will lose them, too.

This book will enlighten you and challenge you to be a better person—and as a result of beginning that new chapter in your life, you'll be able to fulfill God's mission for you, and your purpose for being alive. Of course, simply knowing about your body and mind doesn't glorify God's creation in you. But knowing about them so you can live with His spirit in you gives that body meaning and purpose. One by one we'll take a look at God's plan for you to live a healthy life in body, in mind and in spirit, culminating in a 21-step program to help bring lasting, faith-based changes into your life. Unfortunately, God isn't just a switch that can be "flipped" in your life—you must learn how to invite Him into each moment of your day yourself. My goal is to help you on that journey. Hopefully, by the time you are done with this book, you will have a stronger connection to Him than ever before! God doesn't just show up on your doorstep one day and tell you what your mission is in life. And it does take serious, heartfelt work to form a lasting connection with Him. But remember—you are never alone! He is always there for you, caring for you and guiding your journey. You were created for a purpose, and the more you connect with your Creator, the more you'll understand what that purpose is. Keep this in mind and you'll be in the right frame of mind to begin your work here.

Before we begin addressing each aspect of our lives in isolation, we must understand how they work together. With that in mind, let's begin by taking a look at how our bodies, minds and spirits are influenced by our daily lives, and how they are all essential to our well-being.

Chapter 1

Body, Mind, Spirit:
The Three-Legged Stool

What does it take to have a balanced life? The answer is simple: We must pay attention to our bodies, our minds, and our spiritual life. When we nurture all three, our lives are in perfect balance and harmony. When we neglect any or all of them, we suffer needlessly. Each of the three aspects of our being is a gift from our Creator. Intriguingly, we have been given many clues about how to best nurture each of the three, and yet our Creator seems to have given us the responsibility of figuring out the best ways for each of us to develop in these areas. This book is meant as a guide for Christians and any other interested persons to learn how best to view, to treat, and to develop these three vital parts of who we are.

We live in an era of specialization. Go to the nearest gym and you'll see people who devote themselves, perhaps fanatically, to the pursuit of the perfect physique. Even those of us who don't spend endless hours in a gym think about exercise from time to time…even if we may not do very much of it! We're all aware that diet and exercise are the keys to a healthy body. But we are awash in so much conflicting information about how best to eat and how much to exercise that many of us just throw up our hands and say, "I have no idea what to do!"

How ironic: Two of the biggest industries, each of which generates billions of dollars a year in income, are the fast food industry and the diet and weight loss industry. It seems as though we spend half our lives piling on the pounds and the other half trying desperately to figure out how to lose them. Doesn't sound very balanced to me! And then there's exercise. When some people start to think about exercise, they just lie down and wait until the feeling passes. What's the one thing you hear every time somebody talks about starting an exercise program? You know the words. It's "Consult your physician!" Well, if the whole idea of exercise is to get healthy, and if I have to consult my physician first, then it's probably dangerous! So I'm probably better off not even doing it!

I understand. I've been there myself. I ran track in high school and had the privilege of serving in the United States Marine Corps, so I'm no stranger to exercise. But it's hard for each of us to find the time and the inclination, let alone the best way to add a workout program of any sort to a busy schedule.

Life itself is a privilege. To be alive, to greet the new day, to experience life, to love and be loved…these are all gifts from a loving Creator. But along with the gift of life comes the responsibility for taking care of our bodies, the vehicle in which we travel on this earthly plane. Life's not a lot of fun if our health fails us. And yet so many of us in this society have the idea that others—doctors, hospitals, pharmaceutical companies, to name a few—are responsible for our health.

In reality, there is but one Great Physician, and He gave each of us the responsibility of serving as His main assistant in our time on Earth. If you want to see your primary care physician, take a look in the mirror! We and we alone are responsible for our health, and when we maintain our body through healthy eating and appropriate exercise, we maximize the gifts that God has so freely given to us. Does this mean we have to become fitness fanatics or workout maniacs? Of course not. While we're striving for health, our true goal is balance. Balance means putting our desire for a healthy body and an attractive appearance in its proper perspective. These things are important, but they are just one-third of the overall picture.

In this book, we'll talk about how to find a path that makes sense, in terms of our busy lives and our natural inclinations, to achieve the maximum physical health for which we were intended, in ways that promote our well being, our health, and that elusive concept of balance. The first thing we'll discuss in detail is the concept of how we were meant to take care of our bodies.

Then there's the mind, the second leg, if you will, of the three-legged stool that symbolizes the concept of balance. We need to exercise our bodies…but we also need to exercise and to nourish our minds. Our bodies stop growing by our early twenties, if not sooner. Unfortunately, in our society, so do our minds. Remember the song we sang at the end of each school year when we were little kids? "No more teachers, no more books." Boy, do we take that expression seriously! In our society, all too many of us tend to stop growing mentally even before we stop growing physically.

I think back to the slogan of the United Negro College Fund—A mind is a terrible thing to waste. That expression specifically referred to children born in the inner city who had little or no access to quality education and therefore lacked the opportunity to develop their minds to the fullest. While the tragedy of poor quality education in our inner cities remains a serious matter in our society, what about the minds of people who have full access to educational opportunities…and yet never take full advantage of their God-given ability to think?

The great motivator Zig Ziglar often tells his seminar attendees, "I wish I could sell each of you your brains for $100,000. That way, we'd both be happy. You would value your brain more, because you paid so much for it, and I'd be happy, because I'd have $100,000!"

It's a telling story, but I think Mr. Ziglar dramatically undervalues the potential of the human brain. You and I were each equipped with the same grey matter as Leonardo da Vinci, Ludwig von Beethoven, Albert Einstein, and Bill Gates. Granted, there exists an illusive quality of genius that is bestowed upon only a few in every generation. But are we coming anywhere close to using the amazing minds we have been given? The mind is like a muscle—use it or lose it! In our world, it's all too easy to go through our entire adult lives…without barely having a single new thought! And if we do, we often ignore it. The more you ignore it, the less you'll get.

Most of us tend to live in very well decorated ruts. We drive the same route to the same job, eat the same things at the same places at the same time each day, watch the same shows on TV, say the same things to our kids that we heard our parents say to us, even if we didn't like it when we were on the receiving end, and pretty much go through our entire day without ever turning our minds on and thinking. We don't really have to develop our thinking all that much to have a decent life, but did you really come here for just a decent life? Did our Creator endow us with the mind of a Michelangelo, a Mozart, or a General George Marshall, just to name a few great thinkers, for no purpose?

God gave us minds with the expectation and intense desire that we would go out and use them. The mind is the seat of emotion and decision-making, and we've been expected to think things through, to make choices and decisions, and to recognize God's handiwork and our place in his world. How many of us, however, can honestly say that we have really developed our minds to the fullest?

One of the most corrosive thoughts a human being can have, and all too many of us think this way, is "I know everything I need to know, so why do I need to learn anything more?" If we don't take the responsibility of thinking through how we want our lives to go and how our society should be organized, other people will be make our decisions for us. It's highly unlikely that we will be pleased with the results.

It's incredibly important for us to recognize the gift that our astonishing minds represent, and to shoulder the responsibility to develop our minds to the best of our abilities. How to do that is the focus of the second part of this book.

Finally, we come to the realm of the spirit, the third area that we will address in this book. What does it mean to be a truly spiritual person in our material world? How do we strike a balance between our earthly responsibilities and our divine calling or sense of mission? What are we called to be, and how do we incorporate God's call into our daily lives?

I use the word "incorporate" intentionally, because its root is "corpus" or body, and the challenge we face each day is how to resolve the seeming tension between body and spirit. We tell ourselves that we want to be better people, but the temptation to cut corners is strong, especially in a world where it seems that "everybody's doing it." We have ideals we want to live up to in terms of how we live our lives, but we often trample our ideals in the pursuit of material success. When we engage ourselves in the question of the spirit, we're really asking the question, how do we rise above the trials and temptations of everyday life and connect with the spark of divinity inside each of us?

The great motivator Tony Robbins tells the story of a young man who drove cross-country to San Diego to start a new job. Unfortunately, when he arrived, he discovered that the company that hired him could no longer afford to pay his salary, and the job offer had been withdrawn. He was a resourceful young man, and although he had no friends or acquaintances in the region, he resolved to find a way to make things work. Since his savings were limited, he did something that first night he would never have imagined doing—he slept in his car.

The next day, he woke up, proud of himself for having saved the cost of a hotel room, showered at a local gym, and began seeking employment. For whatever reason, the job search was not immediately successful, and he decided that sleeping in his car wasn't the worst thing in the world. It wasn't ideal, but he was mobile—he could go to the beach, he could go to a park, he could go wherever he wanted in his new "mobile home." He actually spent a considerable period of time in his car before he found regular employment and was thus able to afford a true home of his own.

Robbins tells the story, and I recount it here, to illustrate the principle that when we let go of our standards, we do so slowly, gradually, over a period of time, not all at once. Whatever spiritual standards we may have set for ourselves as young people in church, on our wedding day, or at some other religious setting, don't disappear in a sudden burst. Instead, all too often, our spiritual values can fade over time, like material on a sofa or couch too long exposed to direct sunlight. When we let our standards down, we let ourselves down, and before long, we can end up letting down everyone we care about.

The businesspeople who ran Enron, Tico, WorldCom, and the other companies that today symbolize corporate greed and destructiveness most likely did not set out to create financial success at the expense of thousands or even millions of others. I've never met these individuals, but I'm sure that as young people they began their careers with the intention of living according to spiritual values, which, at its essence, simply means knowing the difference between right and wrong. Over time, though, opportunities arose, temptations presented themselves, and they fell prey to the lesser side of human nature, the part of us that winks at wrongdoing. Before long, the improper activities they conducted behind closed doors became front-page news that led to humiliation for themselves, their companies, and, not least, their loved ones.

When we're talking about spiritual standards, we're not really discussing the creation of standards that never existed before in our lives. Instead, we're talking about getting back to the beliefs that we have always cherished but haven't found the time or the methods by which to integrate them into our lives.

As Christians, we are comfortable with the idea of the Trinity, because it symbolizes our concept of God and the way God revealed himself to the world through his son Jesus Christ. Today, I'm inviting you to take a journey with me to discover another trinity, the trinity of body, mind, and spirit. If our bodies are temples, then how can we continue to pollute and poison them through unhealthy eating practices and lack of adequate exercise? If our minds have the capacity to create symphonies, cathedrals, software programs, and even ultrasound monitors to determine the health of the yet-to-be-born baby, how can we not take full advantage of the marvelous gift of the human brain, with which we have been so generously endowed?

Since we know that God said, "Put first things first," why do we put the chase for material things, property, and prestige ahead of the basic human need to live a rich and meaningful spiritual life? These are the issues I want to explore with you in this book. I want to give you a roadmap for developing balance among these three basic aspects of our nature—a healthy body, a healthy mind, and an activated spirit. When we put first things first, and when we as Christians recognize just what gifts our Father in Heaven has so generously given us, we wouldn't want to wait a single minute to explore these wonderful gifts and develop them to the fullest. That's the challenge that I set forth.

If you want to explore the concept of the healthy body, you can turn first to that section of the book. If you want to learn more about developing the powers of the mind, that section awaits you. And if you want to delve first into matters of the spirit, you can join me right away in the third part. In the fourth section—the closing remarks, I'd like to offer some thoughts about how to integrate our bodies, our minds, and our spirits into a healthy, organic whole.

In my own career as an investment advisor, real estate investor, motivational speaker, and broadcaster, I've seen the best and, yes, the worst of human nature in all its varieties. Together, let's take the first step on the journey toward maximizing the gifts that God has given us. The gifts of physical health, mental strength, and spiritual connectedness, and above all, true balance, await. So let's get going on this all-important quest!

Part I:

The Body

Chapter 2

God Wants You Thin

The Bible tells us that the body is a temple.

But when you look at the bodies of most people, they appear to have spent not enough time in the sanctuary and too much time in the buffet line in the social hall after services.

Life takes energy, and energy comes from running our bodies efficiently. But life is complicated, and despite our best intentions, most of us don't take the time we need to treat our bodies the way we should. We eat the wrong things, and too much of them. We make New Year's resolutions and promises to ourselves to exercise more, to get to the gym, but those promises all too often fall by the wayside as the realities of our time commitments at home and work take priority. We know we need enough sleep, so that our bodies can rest, recover, and rebuild from the stress and tension of the day before. But even adequate sleep is hard to come by in our twenty-four-hour day, technology-driven, fast-paced society.

We don't really "own" our bodies. Everything we are, and everything we have, belongs to God. We are stewards of the wealth and gifts that God has given us, stewards for a lifetime. As believers, it's not just a human body that we're responsible for. It's the godly gift of life, with which we have been entrusted, and we have to take the best possible care of our bodies because God has ordained us to do so.

Without health and energy, who are we? What have we got? What can we do? Of what value are all the great spiritual intentions and inclinations in the world, if we don't have the physical strength to carry out our mission in life? What can we accomplish in our churches, in our homes, in our workplaces, in our society, without the energy and strength to translate our good intentions into right action? How can we perform our Christian walk...if we find ourselves having a hard time getting up off the couch? And what kind of example are we setting through our actions for the next generation? It can't be that great an example, because we are raising the most obese, diabetes-prone generation of young people the world has ever known.

When we don't take care of our bodies, we're not just failing ourselves, we're failing our children, and our Creator. That's too big a burden, and I don't want to live that way. I know you don't, either.

Fortunately, God provided an outstanding health and fitness text for us all to follow. It's called the Bible. Most of us think of the Bible as a guide solely to matters of the spirit. But in reality, the Bible has plenty to teach us about how to take care of our physical selves as well. They must have known something back then, because the luminaries of Genesis—Noah, Methuselah, and others of their time—lived for 600, 700, 800, or 900 years or more. Abraham lived well into his second century, and Moses passed at the advanced age of 120. What did they know about nutrition, exercise, and lifestyle that we have forgotten? Plenty, as it turns out, and in this section of the book, I'd like to share with you an approach to health and fitness grounded in the unimpeachably wise guidance of the Old and New Testaments. Who better than God to create an Owner's Manual for the human body? He designed it, so surely He knows best how to take care of it.

When we buy a new car, we baby it. We make sure we find out the right level of octane it needs to run most efficiently. We change the oil regularly, maintain appropriate tire pressure, and follow the service guidelines set forth in the Owner's Manual. We want the car to have a long life with us, and we also want to preserve its resale value, so that we can derive maximum value at the time we sell it or trade it in.

So it is with our human bodies. When we optimize our nutrition, we are giving ourselves the right fuel. When we provide appropriate maintenance, we are ensuring that we will have long and useful running lives. And we are also guaranteeing that we will have created the foundation for a second life for ourselves, one that will last not just for the three to ten years we own a car but for the eternity we will be privileged to spend with our Creator.

So there's not just a physical imperative to take care of ourselves at least as well as we take care of our automobiles. There's a spiritual imperative as well. God gave us our bodies, and God gave us great direction about how to take care of ourselves. We listen to God's word to govern our spiritual lives. So doesn't it make much sense to see what God has to say about how to run our physical beings as well?

What was the biblical lifestyle, and how did it differ from ours? In early biblical times, most people lived close to the land. Life was much simpler then. There were no trains, planes, and automobiles—if you wanted to get somewhere, you walked. Adequate exercise and movement was a part of every person's day. If you wanted to eat something, you went out and grew it. Or you slaughtered an animal you had raised, as Abraham did when the three visitors—angels disguised as travelers—arrived at his tent in the heat of that long ago Canaan afternoon. The calves that Abraham served his guests were not raised in a "factory farm." They were not pumped full of hormones and drugs designed to make them grow faster and fatter. They were free-range animals. As a result, the meat they provided was healthier than anyone could ask for.

In the mood for wine? In biblical times, you didn't have the convenience of calling up the local liquor store, which might even provide home delivery. When Noah emerged from the arc after forty days and forty nights onboard with his family and wide variety of animal friends, he wanted a nice glass of wine. So what did he do? He planted his own vineyard. The wine he subsequently produced for himself contained no tannins, no preservatives, none of the impurities and imperfections that we find in alcoholic beverages today.

When the Israelites were crossing the desert en route to the Holy Land, they didn't stop into McDonald's for a Happy Meal. When the manna descended from Heaven, God didn't ask, "Do you want to super size that? Do you want fries with it?" They received exactly what they needed, in exactly the right portions. There are few, if any, overeaters in the Bible. How could they be? They didn't have refined sugar, white flour, chemicals, additives, or preservatives. They didn't have to wonder if the food they were eating was genetically modified. The devil has always existed, but you won't find devil dogs in the Bible. You get the point. Back then, people ate in a healthy manner because there were only healthy things to eat.

They also got enough rest. We'll go more deeply into this subject in a later chapter, but your body needs sleep in order to repair the damage experienced during the day. Back then; there was no such thing as electric light, let alone late night TV. Work ended at dark, and people came in from the fields or from tending the livestock to get their rest. They were early risers—especially when there was something important to do. When God commanded Abraham to sacrifice his son Isaac, the Book of Genesis tells us that they rose early in the morning. So did Jacob after he dreamt of the ladder stretching to Heaven with angels ascending and descending. They went to bed early, and they arose early. I'm not telling you that you have to be a morning person in order to be spiritual. I am saying that adequate rest, and living in harmony with the rhythm of nature, was how people lived back then. No wonder they lived such long and contented lives. No wonder they were less prey than we to disease and famine. No wonder they were able to complete their missions of divine service. They had the nutrition, exercise, and therefore the energy to meet God's expectations of them, and their own expectations of themselves.

Fast forward to modern times. We've got choices—we're overwhelmed with choices of what to eat, how much, when, and where. When we're given choices, all too often, we make bad ones, or worse yet, we let other people make our decisions for us. When you're growing up, it *is* your parents' job to tell you to eat your vegetables. But once we become adults, who's telling us what to eat, how much, and when? The media, the food industry, and the restaurant industry. Typically, when you go into a restaurant for a meal, they serve you twice or even three times as much as you might serve yourself if you were preparing your own dinner. Why? Because that way they can charge you the exorbitant prices that many restaurants print on their menus. They couldn't make money serving you the relatively small amount of food we need at any given mealtime. That would kill their bottom line. Unfortunately, all that excess food fills our waistlines. That's because those same parents who told us to eat our vegetables also told us to clean our plates. The problem is that when we go out to most restaurants, our plates are overflowing with food. That's especially the case if we are in an establishment with a buffet, where we feel the financial obligation to maximize our investment in the meal…by taking and eating all the food we can. I wonder if people who lose money in Las Vegas casinos feel they have to take their financial revenge in the all-you-can-eat buffets. Either way, we allow ourselves to be over-served to a radical degree. Any food the body cannot burn up as energy, it stores as fat. So we can't trust restaurants to be our nutritional advisors.

The food manufacturing industry is not much better. They're not in the job of watching out for our nutritional interests. They're in the business of making food taste good, so that we'll buy a lot of it, eat quickly, and then buy more. When the old Lays' potato chip ads told us that, "Bet you can't eat just one," they were making a multimillion dollar bet on our appetite. Unfortunately for us and for our waistlines, and our health in general, they won. Many of us like to see scary movies, and we pay good money at the movie theater or at the video rental store for the latest terrifying releases. But if you want to be really shaken up, it won't even cost you a dime. Just read the nutritional labels on food items at the grocery store. If you aren't scared reading those things, then you aren't paying attention. The problem is that most of us aren't paying any attention at all. The only criterion for whether we're going to eat something is not whether it's good for us—it's just how it tastes. As they used to say at Weight Watchers, Americans are digging their own graves with their forks.

In the Bible, the one thing that never seemed to be lacking was time. You never see a biblical patriarch or matriarch multitasking, stressed out, trying to do too much in too little time, grabbing a meal on the run. Show me a biblical meal that isn't a feast, or at least a healthy repast, and I'll be amazed. Back then; eating was an activity that took place only when all other activities ceased. People weren't sitting at their desks, staring into their computer screens, gobbling down a lunch of dubious nutritional quality that they just purchased from a vending machine. They weren't eating a microwaved bowl of Ramen. They weren't rushing out to a fast food "restaurant" and filling up on starch, sugar, and other empty calories. They weren't overloading on sodium, which modern food producers use as a preservative, and as a means of enhancing flavor—once again—so you'll eat more and eat more often. Instead, in biblical days, a meal was a time to relax, sit with guests, friends, or family and celebrate, but there was no such thing as a "lunch meeting." As a result, people were more conscious about how much food they put in their bodies. We are not like that anymore. We typically have no idea how we ate, where we ate, when we ate, how much we ate, or even why we ate. Were we really hungry? Or were we just stressed or anxious, and we were using food in order to assuage uncomfortable feelings? Perhaps we were watching a movie or a game on TV, and went through an entire dish, pint of ice cream, a bag, or a couple of bags of snacks, without even giving the matter the slightest thought. In other words, a lot of the eating we do today has nothing to do with hunger. For most of us, overeating is a way of life.

Why am I starting a book about body, mind, and spirit with so much emphasis on our eating habits? I'm doing so because we all have responsibilities—to ourselves, our families, employers, clients, society, religious institutions, and to God. If we are going to be of maximum service to those around us and the One who is above us, we must have the energy to do that. If we don't feed ourselves properly, we'll never have the energy to meet all of our responsibilities. We won't enjoy either the quality or quantity of life that the Bible clearly indicates is our heritage. When I say that "God wants you thin," I admit I'm being a little bit tongue in cheek. But really, don't you want your children to be in the best possible health? Don't you wish your kids the blessings of fitness and high energy, so they can go out and conquer the world? Well, God wants the same for His kids, and that means you and me. It's a sin to treat another human abusively. It's a sin to abuse an animal. So why isn't it sinful for us to abuse our own bodies? That's the question I'm posing to you right now.

The word sin itself is an intriguing concept. It's actually a term from archery, and it means, "to miss the mark." When we commit the "sin" of failing to take care of our bodies through proper nutrition, exercise, and rest, we're missing the mark of what life is all about. Businesspeople will tell you that the individual who is in the best physical shape often wins in negotiations, because he has the physical stamina to see the deal through. One of the reasons Tiger Woods is head and shoulders above all the other golfers of his era is because he's in so much better shape than they are. Tiger works out not just on the practice range but in the weight room, which means that he has the strength and stamina to win not just the physical game but the mental game in order to close out his opponents in major tournaments.

Closer to home, marriages founder because couples don't have enough energy for each other. They've both worked all day, inside and outside the home, they've prepared meals for the kids, driven carpool, worked overtime, and by the time the children are asleep, parents find themselves collapsing on the couch, staring mindlessly at some dopey TV show, simply because they don't have the energy to lavish on each other. Lack of energy is the surest way to kill a relationship, and soaring divorce rates, outside and, unfortunately, inside the church, are a sad testament to this fact.

We can't be our best selves if we are not taking the best possible care of ourselves. I wish I had a radical, esoteric, approach that didn't involve making better eating choices, because there's little as unpalatable for most of us than hearing the unsurprising news, that if we eat better, we'll feel better and we'll probably live longer. But that's the way it is.

Anyone reading this book made a decision for Christ a long time ago. In that decision, we committed ourselves to a spiritual way of life, to a belief system, to an approach that told us that if we were willing to forego some of the dubious pleasures of this life, we would find eternal life, that our lives would be meaningful, here and hereafter. The root of the word decision means, "to cut away." When we make a decision, we cut away all the other possible choices that we could have made. We let go of lesser options and we embrace the best choice that we can find. If you were a cigarette smoker and you quit, there was a point when you decided that you had smoked your last cigarette. For me, that moment came in 1969. I smoked my last one and told myself, "Never again." You may have done the same thing. It's not that I didn't want a cigarette the next day or the next month. I could have compromised and told myself, "One cigarette won't hurt me. But that was not an option for me, because I knew I'd be back to a two-pack-a-day habit in no time. Now, almost forty years later, of course, I have no desire for a cigarette, but I can tell you the first few weeks were a challenge for me. When an alcoholic or drug addict makes the decision to give up his addiction and find treatment, there's no such thing as "tapering off." At some point, the recovering alcoholic or addict must back up his decision with action, with the commitment to refrain from prior, unhealthy behavior and live in a brand new way.

That's what I'm asking you to do right now. If you truly want to maximize your usefulness to your family, to your fellows, and to God, you've got to be in the right physical condition to manage those complex and often tiring tasks. If it were easy to be a great parent, a great spouse, and a great worker, everybody would be one. The reality is that little in this life that matters comes easily. The Bible tells us we have to work for what we receive, and if we're going to work, we've got to be prepared. It's not enough to educate our minds and develop our spirit. We've got to start at the beginning. "We must treat our bodies like the temples God created them to be, and healthy living starts with healthy eating. I'm asking you now to make the dramatic decision to make your eating habits every bit as important to you as your prayer habits.

I want to recommend to you an entirely new way to look at your eating habits, because I want you to live well enough and long enough to fulfill the spiritual, familial, and work obligations that you have taken on for yourself. Yes, genetics plays a part in our health, but it's a much smaller part than most of us realize. Our genetics may not be under our control, but our diet surely is, and the way we eat has a huge impact on the quality of our lives. God wants us thin—not painfully thin or absurdly thin, but lean and strong, the way he meant for us to be. God gave us free will, and it's time to exercise that free will in the direction of the healthy lifestyle that we need to embrace, and it all comes down to making a decision.

Whom you decide to marry, whether to have children, who your friends are, what school you go to, what jobs you take—these are all decisions you made and stuck to. I'm asking you to make one of the most important decisions you'll ever make—to change your eating habits so that you can be the person you were meant to be. If you want to do this, the question becomes, where do you begin?

My answer to you is simple: Begin by doing what your neighbors are doing to lose weight.

They're eating a little less at each mealtime—they're eating as much as they need, and no more.

When they go to a restaurant, they don't allow the restaurant to dictate how big a portion they're going to eat. They eat about half of what's on their plate, and then check in with themselves to ask if they really need to keep eating. Then they take the rest home for a meal for the next day. (Not a midnight snack.)

When they're eating, they're not watching TV, driving, working, or staring at a computer screen. They're paying attention to what they eat so they don't unconsciously eat too much.

They're getting the fast food out of their lives, because with the possible exception of the salads, there's practically nothing you can find in a fast food chain restaurant compatible with the healthy lifestyle you want to enjoy.

Whether they eat three meals a day, or five smaller meals a day, or three meals and two snacks, they make healthy choices each time they eat.

They pay attention to the nutritional information on food packaging and avoid products with too much salt, sugar, or fat.

Above all, they make eating a conscious part of their lifestyle instead of a reflexive, unconscious activity that takes place whenever the urge strikes.

I'm not talking about starving yourself beginning some fad diet. I'm also not suggesting that you make a completely radical change and throw out everything in the refrigerator except the broccoli. I am saying that when you first make the decision to eat properly, you get yourself into a process that takes you to your ultimate goal of healthy eating, healthy weight, and a healthy life.

Let's talk about weight loss for a moment. If you're among the tens of millions of Americans who are overweight by a factor of more than five or ten pounds, the first thing to do is to shed that excess weight. There are many proven methods for weight loss to explore. I highly recommend that you adopt a nationally proven program like Weight Watchers, Slim-Fast, Deal-A-Meal, NutriSystem, or other approach that is neither extreme nor a fad diet but instead has proven itself as a healthy means of weight loss. Stick to the program. Most Christians have invited God into their lives to offer direction and guidance, but somehow we never let God into the kitchen. Invite God into this phase of your life now. Ask Him to help you stick to the decision you've made and ask Him to help you stay on the program you have chosen. It's tough to do something like this alone, so see if there are family members of yours, friends, coworkers, or neighbors who might be interested in joining a weight loss program with you. You can make it into something fun—make bets with other people about who's going to lose the most weight in a given amount of time. The combination of cooperation and competition will definitely enhance your commitment to your own weight loss and well-being. Have fun with it, and recognize that by eating in the manner that gives you the greatest health, energy, fitness, and strength, you're doing the work of your Creator just as much as when you are in prayer, reading the Bible, or performing any act of charitable or community service.

The best time to start a program like this is right now. The older we get, the more our metabolism changes and slows down, and the harder it is to lose weight. But weight loss by itself is only a temporary fix. The lifestyle change I advocate in this book is a permanent solution to an ongoing problem. Yes, you might miss the salt, the sugar, and even the flavoring and "mouth feel" that man-made chemicals provide, the kinds of things you most likely have enjoyed in your diet up to now. But by moving away from these unhealthy foods, substances, and eating habits, you'll be moving in the direction that your Creator wants you to go. I hope by now you've come to agree with me that God truly wants you thin, and the future of your health, happiness, and human relationships are all in your hands.

Once you've lost the weight and begun a commitment to eating healthy, it will be time to eat in the manner that God set forth in His ultimate diet and nutrition handbook, the Bible. I've studied carefully all of the references to healthy eating and healthy living that the Bible contains, and I've put them together for you in what I call the Salvation Diet. And you'll find that diet in the next chapter.

Chapter 3

The Salvation Diet

If God wants us thin, then why didn't he write a diet book?

Actually, he did! And it's called the Bible. The Bible offers, through law and example, a highly intelligent, sophisticated way to eat in order to maximize our health and our life spans. In earliest times, the Book of Genesis recounts, people lived for centuries. Noah lived to the age of 950. Adam, 930. Methuselah reached the ripe old age of 969. And other early Biblical figures enjoyed lives that lasted from 365 (Enoch) to 777 years (Lamech).

What were they eating? The Bible doesn't specify exactly what foods these long-lived individuals consumed, but we can be certain that none of them ever sampled anything requiring preservatives, chemicals, additives, or other unnatural things. The meat they ate was unadulterated and came from cows and steers that never knew an injection of bovine growth hormones or other potentially harmful (to the animals and to us) additives and medications. The milk they drank came straight from the cow or goat and did not contain emulsifiers, stabilizing agents, or anything else to maintain its healthfulness on a long journey from the farms to our grocery shelves to our refrigerators. The grain they ate was not stripped of all its nutrients in order to preserve it for days or weeks. Everything they ate and drank was as fresh and delicious as could be. The Biblical lifestyle was one hundred percent organic.

And then for reasons known best to Himself, God decided that the appropriate life span for a human being should be a hundred and twenty years. The best known example of an individual reaching that age in the Bible, of course, is Moses, who spent a third of his life growing up in the Pharaoh's palace, a third in exile after having killed the Egyptian overseer who had struck one of his Israelite countrymen, and a third serving as leader of the Jewish people. For most of his life, Moses ate the same Biblical diet as did his forebears, with the exception of the forty years in the desert, when he and his people at the manna that descended six days a week from heaven, with a double portion on Fridays for the Sabbath. Today, many health experts believe that the human body retains the capacity to live a hundred twenty years. What's the difference between ourselves and our Biblical ancestors? The adulterated food we eat, the polluted water we drink, the dirty air we breathe, the sedentary lives we lead, and the physical, emotional, and mental stress we place upon ourselves. In a different vein, Crosby, Stills and Nash once sang of the importance of "getting back to the garden." In our world, the Garden of Eden to which we would all love to return can be accessed most quickly and easily through discovering and keeping to the diet that our Biblical role models, from Adam and Eve to Jesus, kept. Our nation has the world's best medical facilities, the best doctors, and the most medical knowledge ever gathered in one place in human history. And yet, the average life span of an American today is seventy-four years, not the hundred and twenty promised us in the Bible. Why are we shortchanging ourselves to such a shocking degree? Could we really live forty-six years longer if we took better care of ourselves? The only way to find out is to try to live by the examples set for us in the Bible. They ate well, they worked hard, they prayed and fasted, and they stayed connected to their families and to their God. So should we. But how? How exactly can you eat a diet in keeping with the guidance of the Bible in today's fast food culture?

Changing habits is hard. We all know that. If it were easy to make changes and stick to them, we would all be at the perfect weight for ourselves and we would never be tempted by food that is not beneficial for us.

I'm sure this isn't new news to you. We all know that the Biblical life span was longer than our own, and we all sense that there's something wrong with the modern American diet, given the number of overweight adults and the increasing number of overweight teens and young children in our midst. Many of us have tried to lose weight, and most of us have supported, in one way or another, the multibillion-dollar diet industry in this country. But it shouldn't take a billion dollars for people to lose those extra pounds around the middle. Common sense tells us that putting healthy foods in our body is an important way to make our bodies healthier. But common sense, even combined with willpower, isn't enough to keep the average person lean and fit.

Everybody's looking for a magic bullet that will allow them to eat as much as they want, exercise as little as they want, and have the fabulous body of their dreams. Bad news, people. There's no such thing, no matter how much we might desire or crave it. The road to a healthy body runs, as it always has, through eating less and exercising more. We all know the basics. Eat lean cuts of meat. Eat less. Eat more slowly. Don't drink calories— alcohol, soda, exercise drinks like Gatorade, and even fruit juice contain large numbers of empty calories without helping us meet our nutritional needs or even to feel full.

We all sense there's something suspicious about all those "fat-free" foods that add inches to our waistline. Here's the simple truth: The food may not have any fat in it when you eat it, but all those extra calories *turn* to fat when they nestle into your body with nowhere to go. You'd have to run a half marathon to burn up the energy contained in a box of fat-free cookies. And if you're going to get in the business of half marathons, the last thing you'll want to do is waste all that effort on a box of junk food.

How low can the corporate food industry, working hand in glove with the pharmaceutical industry, go to convince us to eat unnatural, unhealthy things? How about all those ads on TV these days for antacids that you can take *before* you eat the stuff you know you shouldn't be eating, with or without a pill? And take a look at the actors and actresses on those ads. Is there a single one whose body you'd rather have than your own? They're not just trying to sell you pills. They're trying to make you feel good about looking bad. The Bible is full of feasts, from the meal that Abraham served the three angels who came to announce that his wife Sarah would have a child, to the Last Supper, and nobody needed antacids, before or after those meals. When we're talking about the Salvation Diet, we're talking about protecting ourselves and our loved ones from the unhealthy foods that lead to loss of health and shortened life. We've all got a great uncle who smoked, drank, ate red meat, and never exercised and lived to be eighty-seven. But most of us have a lot more relatives who never reached sixty. Why do people die young? Is it strictly a matter of genetics? You and I know better. A healthy life is a choice, which means that in many, many cases, illness is a choice. And it's a choice that God wants you to avoid.

One thing working against all of us is age. As we get older, our metabolisms slow down, which means that it takes longer to burn the same amount of calories compared with the past. When we were in our teens, our twenties, and perhaps even our early thirties, we could "get away" with pizza at two in the morning, big plates of appetizers, and hefty desserts. By the time we reach our forties, fifties, and beyond, every calorie counts... and counts against us. At the same time, the older we get, the less active we tend to be. Granted, there are individuals running marathons and triathlons into their fifties, sixties, and beyond, but those are rare exceptions. For most of us, the older we get, the more attractive we find the couch instead of the gym, the drive-thru at the fast food restaurant and the salad bar. Combine a slowing metabolism with reduced exercise, and all of a sudden, to turn the advertising slogan upside down, a waist becomes a terrible thing to mind.

Fortunately, there is an alternative to gaining weight and harming our health due to what has become the standard American diet. And it's not just going on yet another diet that relies on processed food or other unhealthy meals or snacks. We all know that diets don't work—that if we're fortunate to lose weight, by eating less, by eliminating certain foods from our diet, or by any other means, healthy or unhealthy, we end up gaining it all back…and more. Typically, diets tend to create a deep sense of hunger for the foods we're not permitting ourselves to eat. Before long, we're in deep trouble, craving the foods we miss so badly that we end up binging on them. And once we start binging, we tell ourselves that we failed yet again, thus giving ourselves permission to continue to eat badly. All those hard-lost pounds reappear on our bodies, reinforcing the sense that we'll never lose weight.

I've got a different way for you to go. The individuals whose lives were recorded in the Bible certainly had access only to healthy food, and because they were shepherds, nomads, or, like Paul, constantly on the go, they were getting plenty of exercise. But they had one more factor in their favor—they deeply believed and trusted God in every aspect of their lives. G.O.D. most emphatically does *not* stand for "Go On a Diet." Many of us take God into our personal lives, asking Him for direction as to how to be the best possible husband, wife, father, mother, son, or daughter. Many businesspeople bring God into their business affairs, asking for His blessing as they go forth each day, trying to live their ethical and spiritual commitment not just on Sundays at church but Monday through Friday at the office as well. People who invite God into their lives, both personal and professional, overwhelmingly report favorable results. So the question naturally arises: Why don't we ask God for help with more things? Specifically, why don't we ask God for help with food?

It might sound silly, until you consider the results attained in the twelve-step program called Overeaters Anonymous or OA. This program is modeled on Alcoholics Anonymous, the granddaddy of all twelve-step programs. What's the secret behind these programs? In AA, the alcoholic knows he cannot stay sober by himself, but with the help of God and his fellows, he can, a day at a time. By analogy, in Overeaters Anonymous, members recognize that they cannot maintain a healthy relationship with food unless they ask God to direct their eating habits. It might sound crazy, but it works—and tens of thousands of overeaters and binge eaters, along with others suffering from other types of eating disorders, have found recovery. The key in all this is a reliance on God.

If you think that God is too busy to care about what you eat, then the good news is that you're sadly mistaken. Those of us who are parents want the best for our children. We want them to make healthy choices in every aspect of their lives, food included. There isn't a parent on the planet who would knowingly subject his or her beloved children to a lifetime of obesity, diabetes, or other food-related illnesses. Just as we want the best for our children, so God wants the best for us. But as the expression goes, God is a gentleman and He doesn't go where He isn't invited. How do you break the cycle of weight loss followed by weight gain? How do you put an end to the yo-yoing of one's weight? There's only one answer, and it's got nothing to do with a fad diet. It's got everything to do with prayer.

I'm going to share with you an approach to eating that works, because it is rooted in principles of health *and* faith. It combines the wisdom of the Bible with cutting edge research about the healthiest way for us to feed ourselves and our children. But I can guarantee you that even the Salvation Diet is doomed to failure if you aren't taking advantage of what I call the secret ingredient—the humble request to God that he help us eat properly, eat the right things, eat the right amounts, and eat ourselves healthy instead of eating ourselves sick. It works for the people in Overeaters Anonymous, individuals of all faiths who have come to recognize and rely on God as the ultimate nutritionist, if you will. So the first tenet of the Salvation Diet is to take God into your eating life the same way you take Him into every other aspect of your life. Each morning, ask Him to direct your eating habits. We can't be of maximum service to God if we are not maximizing our own health and fitness. It takes energy to do anything of importance in this world, from raising a child to building a church, from making a living to making a life. If you still think this sounds silly, try it for thirty days. Ask God each morning to keep you on the right path with your eating. And watch the results.

The Salvation Diet—What Do You Eat?

The late, great syndicated columnist Mike Royko once set forth what he called the Royko Diet—anything you want, you can't have, and anything you don't want, you can have all you want. It's clever, but it obscures the essential truth that most of us have become so comfortable eating the wrong stuff that our bodies have forgotten how good real food tastes. Perhaps the simplest way to practice the Salvation Diet, after you're taking God in as your partner on the deal, is to visit the supermarket and stick to what is served on the perimeter walls. Typically, that's where you find fruits, vegetables, meat, poultry, dairy, seafood, fresh salads, and freshly baked goods. What do you find on the interior of supermarkets? All the processed foods—the snacks, the cookies, the candies, the sodas, everything that's loaded with chemicals and preservatives so it will last on the supermarket shelf and in your pantry before you put it into your system. Stick to the outside walls, and your diet will approximate to a striking degree the way people ate in Biblical times. Consider the Bible verses that discuss food. It's written in Genesis, 1:29, "And God said, 'Behold, I have given you every herb-bearing seed, which is upon the face of the Earth, and every tree, the fruit of the tree yielding seed.'"

That's the fresh fruit department.

And in Ezekiel, 4:9, it says, *"Take wheat and barley, beans and lentils, millet and spelt. Put them in a storage jar and use them to make bread for yourself."* There's the bakery section of your supermarket. Keep away from the white flour—it's a highly addictive substance that puts pounds on the body and offers no nutritional value. The famous ad says that Wonder Bread helps bodies grow in twelve ways. What it ought to say is that it helps make bodies grow fat in one way—because white flour turns to fat in the system of every human being. So stick to the fresh, healthy bread, and you'll be okay.

Then we turn to Daniel, 1:12, where he says, *"Give us nothing to eat but vegetables to eat and water to drink."* There's the vegetable section.

In the mood for meat? Take a look at Genesis, 9:3, where it says, *"Every moving thing that liveth shall be meat for you."* Or Luke, 15:11–32, where you find the parable of the prodigal son, for whom the fatted calf is killed.

If you're looking for a Biblical reference to fish, try Luke, 24:42—*"And they gave him a piece of broiled fish."*

I think you get my point. The perimeter of the supermarket is where you find the foods that most closely resemble the things our Biblical ancestors ate. They lived to a hundred and twenty; if we're lucky, we live to seventy-four. You don't have to have a Ph.D. from Cal Tech to do that math.

The Bible certainly gives many examples of feasts and provides us with some sense of the menus. The Bible also offers instructions as to what types of meat are acceptable. At Deuteronomy, 14:4–5, we learn that the ox, the sheep, the goat, the deer, the gazelle, the roe deer, the wild goat, the ibex, and the antelope were all acceptable dishes for the Israelites of the time. We believe that shellfish is just as acceptable today as is meat, so we can enjoy that as well. The main thing to know is that the Bible speaks frequently of food, because it was just as important a part of the lives of Biblical figures as it is in our lives today. In fact, here is a comprehensive list of specific food items mentioned in the Bible.

Almonds (Genesis 43:11)
Apple (Genesis 2:17)
Apricots (Proverbs 25:11)
Barley (Judges 7:13)
Beans (Ezek. 4:9)
Beef (1 Kings 4:22,23)
Bread (1 Samuel 17:17)
Broth (Judges 6:19)
Butter (from churning milk) (Proverbs 30:33)
Cakes (2 Samuel 13:8)
Cheese (Job 10:10)
Cucumbers, onions, leeks, melons, and garlic (Numbers 11:5)
Curds of cow's milk (aka yogurt) (Deut. 31:14)
Dates (Psalm 92:12)
Eggs (Luke 11:9, 11-13)
Figs (Numbers 13:23)
Fish (Matthew 7:10)
Fowl (1 Kings 4:23)
Fruit (2 Samuel 16:2)

Game (Genesis 25:28)

Garlic (Numbers 11:5)

Goat's milk (Proverbs 17:27)

Grain (Ruth 2:14)

Grapes (Deut. 23:24)

Grasshoppers, locusts, and crickets (Lev. 11:22)

Herbs (Exod. 12:8)

Honey (Isa. 7:15) and wild honey (Ps. 19:10)

Lentils (Genesis 25:34)

Meal (Matthew 13:33)

Mellon (Numbers 11:15)

Nuts (Genesis 43:11)

Pistachio nuts (Genesis 43:11)

Oil (Proverbs 21:17)

Olives (Deut. 28:40)

Pomegranates (Numbers 13:23)

Quail (Numbers 11:32)

Raisins (2 Samuel 16:1)

Raisins (2 Samuel 16:1)

Rye (Ezek 4:9

Salt (Job 6:6)

Sheep (Deut. 14:4)

Sheep's milk (Deut. 32-14)

Spices (Genesis 43:11)

Veal (Genesis 18:7-8)

Vegetables (Proverbs 15:17)

Vinegar (Numbers 6:3)

Wheat (Deut 32:14; Ezek 4:9)

Wine (John 4:46; I Timothy 5:23)

You can't find anything on this list that contains refined or processed carbohydrates, trans fats, or artificial sweeteners. Once we start tasting real food, we realize just how satisfying and delicious these items are. Scientists work overtime at the corporate food producers to come up with ultimately unhealthy things that have great "mouth feel," regardless of how much sugar, fat, or chemicals they contain. But when you go back to what God created, you are putting yourself on the road to health and longevity. Compare the number of calories in an apple with the number of calories in a slice of apple pie. One apple by itself is generally satisfying—it's the perfect portion size. But if you have a slice of apple pie, it's hard to say no to the second slice, to the vanilla ice cream, or even the cheese that accompanies it. I know—I'm making you hungry just thinking about it! But it's the difference between consuming 80 calories and perhaps 800. It would be great if our bodies could feel nourished and full on just two slices of apple pie a day. But you and I know that's not how the game works.

I don't want to get into the debate over what specific foods you should or should not be eating. For every argument, it seems, there is a counter argument. Some people say that you need to eat dairy in order to increase your calcium intake. Others say that dairy products actually strip calcium from your bones, and the best thing to do is to avoid dairy altogether and instead take a calcium supplement. Whatever you're eating, the rule of thumb on the Salvation Diet is moderation. Millions of Americans went on the Atkins Diet, the most famous of the high protein, no carb diets. Why did the Atkins Diet work, at least initially, for so many? Because when you eliminate the carbs from a diet, you eliminate practically all the water from the human body. The initial weight loss that people experienced on Atkins had to do with the amount of water their systems were wringing out. Why does the Atkins Diet ultimately fail for most people? Because the human body simply cannot survive without an adequate supply of water. That shouldn't come as a surprise, but it did, especially to those whose health actually suffered because of their reliance on proteins and fats to the exclusion of carbs.

Another argument into which I will not enter is the question of what percentage of protein, carbs, and fats a person needs. This is something you can take up with your doctor or a nutritionist. I will say, however, that balance and moderation are the key here as well. Our bodies all need protein, whether we derive it from red meat, chicken, rice and beans, or even vegetables. (Many vegetables contain large amounts of protein.) Some argue that we do not need to eat extra amounts of protein, because our bodies create enough protein to meet our needs. I'm not weighing into that one. I'm simply here to say that striking a moderate balance among protein, carbs, and fats is the best way to go.

What about the "food pyramid" that the U.S. Government promotes? Keep in mind that the food pyramid was bought and paid for by corporate food sponsors. Do you really need as much dairy or grain as they say? By the way, whoever said that we had to have cereal and milk for breakfast? That's certainly not one of the commandments that came down on Mt. Sinai! The main thing is to take a look at every piece of information you get about food with a jaundiced eye, even what I tell you! The only place you'll find the "gospel truth"…is in the gospel. Everything else remains suspect.

So far, we've seen in the Salvation Diet that it takes bringing God into the equation to make the whole thing work. Then we saw that sticking to the perimeter of the supermarket puts us in contact with the basics of the diet on which our Biblical forebears thrived. Then we saw that moderation is the key to all things. Salvation doesn't come from stuffing ourselves with food—instead, we have to stop when we're feeling "full enough." And you might have been told, growing up, that you had to clean your plate because of the starving children in some far-off land. But it doesn't do you or the starving children any good to clean your plate. Be especially careful in restaurants, where we are served double or even triple the amount of food we need, in order that restaurants justify the margins they are charging for food.

If you're at a restaurant, don't hesitate to take half of the food on your plate and pack it up in a doggy bag. No one at your table is really going to care. And if they do ask, you can be a positive influence on them as well.

How often should you eat on the Salvation Diet? It's your call. For most of us, three large meals a day really isn't the healthiest approach to eating. This practice was instituted at a time when most Americans worked in factories and went home for lunch at noon. They were by their machines all day, so they did not have access to food from the time they left the house until the time they went home, regardless of peaks or troughs in their blood sugar levels. Today, we know better. If you want to know how often to eat, consider what most successful athletes and trainers do. Instead of three large meals a day, they eat four or five or even six smaller meals. It's okay to break the taboos that keep most of us larded with fat. One of them is, as I mentioned a moment ago, the need to eat only cereal and milk, and perhaps some juice and toast, for breakfast. What about a healthy shake instead? What about some chicken and salad? You might be saying, "Oh, I never eat that for breakfast!" Well, there's a first time for everything!

Breakfast truly is the most important meal of the day, and it is the foundation of the Salvation Diet. The name breakfast itself gives us a clue as to its importance. We're literally breaking the fast—we haven't eaten since the night before, and we're hungry! When you eat a healthy but not overly substantial breakfast, you're not only giving your body the energy it needs to get the day started right, but you're signaling your body that it can relax in the knowledge that you're going to provide it with healthy portions of food as necessary all day long. When we skip breakfast, we tell ourselves that "We're on a diet," when in reality we're just too busy to take good care of our health—we're sending our bodies a very negative and dangerous signal. We're telling our bodies that there isn't enough food to go around, that it may be hours before it sees anything at all nutritious, so it better hunker down and preserve whatever calories it still has remaining to be burned. When we don't eat breakfast, our metabolism slows and we end up in an unhealthy, unbalanced state. By the time the snack wagon rolls around at 10:30, we're just dying for food, and whatever standards we might have had about our eating habits drop off as quickly as do our blood sugar levels. Skipping breakfast and then eating an unhealthy pastry or muffin at mid-morning is a recipe for weight gain, low mood, and poor performance on the job and at home. And it just sets us up for a bigger binge later in the evening.

The alternative on the Salvation Diet: Eat a good breakfast. Eat three meals and two healthy snacks or eat five meals. Don't let yourself get too hungry and don't let yourself get too full. It takes a little more effort to keep fruit around than it does muffins or cake, but your body will replay you grandly for the effort you make in terms of better performance and quicker weight loss. As the great motivator Anthony Robbins says, "Nothing tastes as good as being thin feels."

If you want to take your eating habits a step up, don't just eat anything on the perimeter of the supermarket. Only choose vegetables and fruits grown organically, so as to reduce or even eliminate the level of pesticides that you are taking into your body. Insist on free-range chicken, meat, and eggs, because only then will you avoid some of the health risks associated with meat from animals grown and slaughtered in the traditional manner. Again, the meat we eat today is different from the fresh, healthy meat that they ate in the Bible. It's an open secret that animals raised for slaughter are treated poorly, living in small spaces, often unable to move about freely, and they are shot full of growth hormones and other drugs—which end up in *your* system. This is not exactly a recipe for health, which is why it is vital to opt for free-range chicken, meat, and eggs, even if it costs a little more. It's cheaper than a trip to the doctor!

The subject of healthy versus unhealthy meat triggers one of the most important questions about food in the Bible—did God intend us to be vegetarian? Only after the Flood were human beings allowed to partake of meat. The Old Testament is full of the rules and regulations about what kind of animals may be eaten, how the blood must be poured on the ground, because blood is symbolic of life, and the many feasts at which meat was consumed. By the time of the New Testament, Christians had begun to move away from the laws of kashrut that applied to the Jews of the Bible (and still obtained among many Jewish people today). Many individuals in contemporary society swear by the health benefits of a non-meat diet. They are able to obtain their protein from other sources—nuts, seeds, rice and beans, and vegetables, as mentioned earlier. By avoiding meat, they avoid taking in all of those medicines and chemicals given to animals, and some will even argue that they are healthier because they are not ingesting the souls of slaughtered animals. That might be a bit too much for most of us to accept, but the reality is that a strong case can be made for the vegetarian lifestyle. I don't include vegetarianism as part of the Salvation Diet, because there are too many references in the Bible to lead me to believe that God does not want us to eat meat. But if God were to speak today, I'm sure he'd have plenty to say about the way we treat animals raised for consumption. So you'll have to make your own call on that one.

Fasting is another Biblical practice that remains in vogue today. The Israelites of ancient times, as well as modern Jews, kept regular fast days as part of their religious calendar and also fasted in times of distress, as when Jonah went to prophesize at Ninevah. Fasting is an excellent way to clean out the system and give our internal organs a much-needed reset. Processing all that food, day after day, year after year, is a lot of work for our insides! A half-day fast, a daylong fast, a water fast, a juice fast—these can all be excellent tools in order to cleanse our systems. As always, the key is moderation, because you don't want to go too long without providing your body the nutrition it needs.

What about wine? Practically every religious festival described in the Old and New Testaments begins with blessings pronounced over wine. Drinking spirits has always been considered an accepted way to lift one's spirits. Yet even three thousand years ago, King Solomon wrote disparagingly of those who tarried too long at the wine table, and the way he described the physiology and remorse of a person lapsing into drunkenness rings true today. Many of us find ourselves intrigued by what is called the "French paradox"—the fact that in France, the diet contains heavy fats and oils, and yet the French people often remain quite thin. The missing ingredient in all this turned out to be wine, which, consumed in moderation, is said to have many health benefits. Again, the key word is moderation. Anyone with a tendency toward alcoholism should not use Biblical references to the drinking of wine as an excuse for perpetuating his or her disease. Cirrhosis of the liver, cancer, and many other unfortunate diseases are the result of overindulging in wine.

The final element of the Salvation Diet is the simplest, purest beverage of all, water. Most of us go through our days moderately to severely dehydrated. We gain weight because we think we're hungry...when we're actually just thirsty. Many of us are addicted to caffeinated beverages, like coffee or non-herbal tea. Such beverages are actually diuretics—they leach water out of our system. (That's why we have to go to the bathroom so quickly after we drink coffee as opposed to drinking water!)

The trouble with soda or even fruit juice is that such beverages contain high levels of calories, and the sugar in those beverages does no good for our systems, either. Your body simply needs a great deal of water all day long. How much? For the average adult, eight glasses, each of eight ounces, is a good start. It makes sense to carry around with you or keep next to you at your desk a two-liter bottle of water. Get in the habit of drinking all the water you can. The main element in the composition of our bodies is water, so it stands to reason that replenishing water in our systems is a vital way to keep ourselves healthy and to flush out toxins that otherwise accumulate in our systems. The importance of water goes all the way back in recorded history to the Book of Genesis, where stories of digging wells and finding pure water abound. Genesis also tells the story of Abraham's servant Eliezer, whose strategy for locating a wife for his master's son Isaac was to go to the wells of a city in the early evening, when the daughters of the city came forth to draw water. I'm not saying that water is going to replace singles bars or dating websites as a means of meeting people, but it's certainly a great way to keep yourself healthy while you're looking for a relationship or if you're in one!

So there you have it—the Salvation Diet. Ask God for help every day. Stick to the perimeter of the supermarket and "upgrade" to organic and free-range whenever possible. Avoid processed foods that you cannot find in the Bible, drink plenty of water, eat many small meals throughout the day, never skip a meal, and never let yourself get too "stuffed." Follow these simple directions and you'll save yourself from a lifetime of health issues, and the weight will drop off you in a healthy, surprisingly easy way. God wants you thin and the Bible is His diet book. Now you know what the patriarchs knew about eating right. As you gain in knowledge, you'll lose on the scale, and that's the best earthly reward of all. Next, let's take a look at how you can make fitness a regular, manageable part of your life, and be as healthy as God wants you to be!

Chapter 4

God-Robics

The night before I began writing this chapter, a friend of mine called and asked if I'd take him to the emergency room. His doctor told him that the pain my friend was experiencing in his chest and left arm, and his shortness of breath, were markers for angina, or a heart attack. We went to our local hospital, where he was immediately given an EKG and other tests. The tests quickly revealed that he had in fact suffered some damage to his heart muscle and he was quickly admitted and brought to the ICU. Further testing that night and the next morning proved that he had suffered a heart attack, and over the next three days, he had two separate angioplasties, each to repair the valves on each side of his heart.

There's a happy ending to this story. Although, my friend is forty-six year old, far too young, in my opinion, to suffer a heart attack, he is young enough to make meaningful and substantial changes to his lifestyle. When he comes out of the hospital, it is my strong hope that he will substantially improve his diet, drop the excess twenty-five pounds, start a healthy exercise program, reduce his stress, and take whatever steps necessary in order to lower his unhealthy cholesterol levels and protect his heart and his overall health. He's a smart guy and I'm sure he'll do all of the above.

The point of the story, and the reason that I share it with you here, came about during brief conversation I had with the cardiologist on my friend's first night in the ER. The cardiologist, a man who appeared to be in his mid-fifties, had a lean, trim body. I asked him what he did in order to stay in shape.

He paused, as if surprised by the question. And then he responded with a smile, "Diet and exercise. That's the only magic formula."

Far too many millions of Americans live lives of high stress combined with poor diet and little to no exercise. While it's true that many of us are living longer than ever, paradoxically, many more of us are encountering diseases and conditions at young ages—diseases that are usually associated with older people. I am not trying to scare you into the idea of getting an exercise program?. I can tell you that my friend in the hospital has now been galvanized into taking better care of himself. It shouldn't take a trip to the ER for us to realize the simple truth that if we ignore our bodies; they're going to go away.

Most illness develops for months or even years before it evidences itself in terms of a heart attack, a stroke, or any other life-threatening condition, just as we harbor a cold or flu inside our bodies for a period of time before symptoms evidence themselves. In other words, we don't *have* a heart attack, as if it were a sudden bolt of lightning striking our systems. Instead, we *develop* a heart attack, or any other serious or life-threatening condition, over time. Marathoners don't simply wake up one morning and decide to run a marathon. They train and prepare, through diet and exercise, for months before the race. Conversely, all too many of us are training and preparing our bodies not for the excitement of a marathon but instead for the terror and potential tragedy of the onset of heart disease, cancer, or any of the other afflictions we face. Diet and exercise prepare people for healthy lives. Poor diet and no exercise prepare people for disease and even early death. What are you preparing yourself for at this moment?

I'd like to ask you a very different question right now. Why are you here? Why are you on Earth? Why have you been granted a body, a mind, and a soul? The Bible teaches us that nothing happens by chance. You did not come into this world by chance. You came here for a specific mission—to live in the world of your Creator, to serve Him in truth, to share His love with those around you and your family, your church, your community, your workplace, and your society. That's the business for which you were created. And the body you were given is, essentially, your company car! It's the vehicle by which and through which you are able to live your life, experience God's love, and share it with others.

We get so caught up in focusing on the day-to-day challenges and crises that we forget just how wondrously and miraculously we are made. We think more about how we're going to pay off the credit card bill than the truly miraculous way in which we have been constructed. If we were to spend just a moment thinking about how extraordinary it is that we breathe oxygen into our lungs, that the oxygen becomes nourishment that is sped throughout our bodies by miles of arteries, veins, and capillaries that we did nothing consciously to create, that we are able to enjoy the taste of food, extract energy from it, and excrete the rest, without any conscious thought on our part...that we are constructed for recreation, for procreation, for hard physical work and intense mental effort...if we gave the miracle of our bodies even one one-hundredth of the thought that we devote to our problems, we would never have an unhappy moment in our lives.

But instead, we take our bodies for granted. We accept aging as a passive process, an inevitability that we can neither stave off nor even modify. We spend a lot of time thinking about who we are, but we spend almost no time thinking about what we are. Who are we? God's kids, on a mission to better our own lives and the lives of those around us, through thought, prayer, and deed. What are we? Flesh and blood, muscle and bone, sinew and tissue. The pinnacle of creation. A computer more powerful, complex, and miniaturized than anything Silicon Valley can produce. A machine more durable and rugged than any vehicle that Detroit or Japan could bring to market. A being with the ability to heal itself of everything from cuts and scrapes to broken bones and even to emotional problems like depression and grief. God knew what He was doing when He created us. So what are we doing with the bodies He so graciously bestowed upon us?

In most cases, not enough! As always, the first place to turn for guidance about how to live today is the Bible, because it showed us how those individuals whose minds were uncluttered by television, the Internet, and popular culture lived in a manner consonant with God's desires and intentions for them. In Biblical times, life was lived outdoors. There were no desk jobs! The world of the patriarchs was agrarian, and they tended flocks, made their living fishing and mending nets, raised crops, or otherwise lived on and from the land. They didn't need health clubs, gyms, or personal trainers because they were active all day. They didn't have cable or satellite TV, so they typically went to bed after it grew dark and arose early. The first runner in the Bible? Abraham, who ran to serve the three angels who had come to tell him that he and his wife Sarah, though already elderly, would have a child within the year. The first weightlifter? Jacob, who lifted a massive stone off the cover of a well to demonstrate the intensity of his newfound love for Rachel. The first pitcher? David, who slew Goliath with five smooth stones (and no warm-up tosses). By the way, how do you know that baseball is the first sport mentioned in the Bible? Because Genesis starts, "In the Big Inning!"

All kidding aside, the men and women of the Old and New Testaments unanimously lived lives of great physical activity. We don't. Our bodies were constructed for motion, and yet we spend most of our time sitting—behind a desk, on our couch, in our cars or on public transportation. Health requires energy, and energy, for human beings, derives from motion. When we talk about exercise, the subject just sounds too dreary to discuss. But when we talk about getting moving, then we are following in the footsteps of our Biblical forebears, we're getting healthier as a byproduct, and we're living our lives the way God intended us to live them—by maximizing the use of our physical gifts, instead of letting them waste away.

As you read these words, I don't know if you're young, old, or somewhere in the middle. I don't know if you're a "gym rat" or exercise-averse. I do know that one of the hardest things for people contemplating an exercise program for the first time, or for the first time in a long time, is that we often have so much fear related to the subject.

People who are the most overweight are the least likely to go to a gym, because it's frankly embarrassing to be in a setting where everyone else seems so fit and trim. And the other problem with gyms and health clubs is that it's hard to know what to do, how often, or for how long. Whose exercise program do you follow? What do you concentrate on first? And how do you add exercise to your life in a way that is going to help you and not hurt you? Before we start talking about what sorts of exercise or movement might appeal to you, let's first create a stronger sense of the importance of physical fitness in our lives. As the expression goes, "The employee knows how, but the boss knows why." If we're going to be the bosses of our own health care, if we are going to play the role of primary healthcare provider in our lives, which we surely are, then we have to know why we want to take steps to become healthier. In other words, what's in it for us?

Weight loss boils down to the simple equation of calories in versus calories out. A calorie is simply a measure of energy. When we consume more calories than we need in order to provide us with the energy for the day, those excess calories are stored as fat on our bodies. If you try to put too much fuel in the gas tank of your car, an automatic shutoff valve will thwart the process, or you'll end up with gasoline on the ground next to your tire. Unfortunately, for most of us, our bodies don't have those sorts of shutoff valves. Most of us eat much more than we need. More calories in and fewer calories expended equals weight gain. When we exercise, we burn calories. It's that simple. The more exercise we get, the more calories we burn, and the first thing that happens is that our weight starts to head south instead of north. My doctor told me to get at least 30 minutes of "exercise" every day to burn calories and improve your muscles which is the "engine" that burns calories. Calories in the form of food is like gas to an engine. What would happen if you keep filling your tank every day but failed to start your engine. Well, you would have to find a place to store that extra gas until it's needed. The body has the ability to store unused energy in the form of fat. And fat creates a national health problem called obesity. For the sake of simplicity I want to address this problem of obesity or being over weight.

From my own observation I don't see fat people in concentration camps. Usually they are thin and gaunt looking. They don't have a problem with weight just with their health. So the relationship between food intake and obesity is obvious. The flip side of obesity is anorexia which results when a person starves them selves. Also one of the medical methods of loosing weight is called "the band" where a band is inserted to limit the food intact into your stomach. You are therefore limited to eating very little. The result is weight loss. So there is a balance and need to eat only what's needed to maintain weight and remain healthy. I am not giving medical advice here, just using common sense from my God created mind. God does provide answers to prayer and they are usually filtered through your brain.

Diets you ask??? I remember being on a 30-day diet once. It was the latest fad diet. What did I loose? I lost a month. Let's move on.

Financial Obesity; I insert this little diversion because being in debt and not having enough income to cover it can create stress in your life. I want you to understand that stress, like excessive weight, is counter to good health. Stress kills because the stress is not limited to one area of your body. Stress attacks your entire system and can cause serious problems. So, Financial Obesity is a new term which refers to an overweight financial balance. You are spending more than you are taking in. Like too much food there must be a place to put this excess debt because it doesn't just disappear. It keeps building until you stop doing it. The excess shows up on your negative balance sheet and internally through unhealthy stress. Like the solution to loosing weight you must break he habit and stop the excessive intake of more debt. Those with too much debt are tempted to respond to advertisements who offer quick solutions to your problem. The advertisers tell you they can have you debt free in 5 years. Pay off your mortgage and your credit cards etc. in record time and they will show you how if you will just hire them. Save your money. The principals are always the same because you can't pay off your 30-year mortgage in 5 years unless you make very large payments every money. The extra payments reduce your balance and eliminate years of interest.

Instead of making minimum payments on your credit cards make double and triple payments. Forget about eating out, taking trips or entertainment. Get a second job and start writing bigger checks to your creditors. There is no "magic" in being debt free. Break the debt habit and operate on a cash basis whenever you can. Follow this advice and thank me later. You can do this your self. Financial Obesity is a killer. Getting rid of debt will extend your life and the quality of your life.

Exercise doesn't have to be strenuous in order to be useful. In fact, strenuous exercise is the exact opposite of what an overweight person needs. There are health risks associated with overly strenuous exercise, especially for an individual who has not worked out a great deal in the past. As always, check with a physician prior to starting any weight loss or exercise program. Henry David Thoreau once wrote, "Beware of any activity that needs new clothes." The same thing could be said of athletic endeavors, at least for those who are getting into an exercise program for the first time. The simplest activities, the activities for which our bodies were designed, are often the most profitable when it comes to getting fit. If you're trying to lose weight, walking is actually better for you than running in most cases. That's because when we walk, our heart rate is elevated into a fat burning zone. When we run, our heart rate goes up higher than the fat burning zone and gives us great cardiac benefits but does nothing for our waistlines. You've probably got a decent pair of sneakers—a pair you wear every day, or a pair hiding at the bottom of the closet. They're all you need to get started.

Similarly, swimming is a fantastic exercise because it places no stress on your knees or ankles, you can do it at practically any age, and you generally don't get your heart rate high enough in swimming to move out of the fat burning zone. If you haven't swum in awhile, you might consider hiring a swimming coach for a couple of one-hour sessions to teach you the latest techniques. Swimmers today move much more efficiently through the water than they did ten or twenty or thirty years ago. If you're going to exercise, why not make the experience as efficient and enjoyable as possible?

The same is true whether you are swimming or doing anything else. Why do Olympic records continue to fall? Because elite athletes have better training programs and better nutrition than in the past. The same lessons that elite athletes are learning about how to succeed in their sports are often applicable to "weekend warriors" and regular folks who are just trying to sneak in a workout here and there. It's a great thing to work out with a personal trainer, if you can afford to do so, because you will receive all kinds of challenges to your body. You'll have a knowledgeable partner who can create a program tailored to your needs and aspirations. Additionally, you'll enjoy companionship when you work out, which makes a big difference— not all of us are cut out to go to the gym and work out alone, although some people really enjoy that. And you'll gain a wealth of knowledge about what your body needs and how to help yourself achieve your fitness goals.

Sometimes people are afraid that they could injure themselves exercising. That's why it's important not to bite off more than you can chew—not to try to lift as much weight on a weight machine at the gym as the guy next to you, because he may well have been working out for years. At a minimum, he knows how to use the machine properly, so as not to get hurt! There's nothing to stop you from running marathons eventually, but the best way to start an exercise program, or anything else for that matter, is to create reasonable goals for yourself. If you've never run a mile, make your first goal to walk a quarter mile, and work your way up. If you've never biked for half an hour, or if you haven't done that since childhood, start at ten minutes and work your way up. A couple of laps in the pool is a great beginning, and before you know it, you'll be swimming lap after lap, effortlessly. I can't promise that if you exercise, you'll never injure yourself. You can take proper precautions, like working with a trainer or a knowledgeable friend, in order to maximize your safety in the gym.

You also have to know and respect your own limits—people typically get hurt only when they push themselves past the level of endurance that they know they possess. But there's nothing that says that you are bound to get hurt if you exercise. The overwhelming majority of non-professional athletes have never seriously injured themselves exercising, because they stay within the limits they set for themselves or that their trainers set for them. You don't have to go from zero to Olympic-caliber overnight! But for every seemingly fit thirty-five-year-old who drops dead of a coronary occlusion on the tennis court, there are thousands upon thousands more individuals his age who are courting heart disease, cancer, stroke, diabetes, and early death by failing to maintain even the simplest of athletic regimens.

How should you begin? Let's first talk about the two different kinds of exercise out there. Aerobic exercise is where you build your cardiovascular system—your heart and your lungs. This includes walking, running, bicycling, swimming, and other activities that involve your whole body, or at least your legs, in constant motion. Then you have anaerobic exercise, which includes weightlifting and the use of weight machines. Anaerobic exercise builds muscle mass and gives you added strength, balance, and bone density. Which should you do, aerobic or anaerobic exercise? Both! And no one's too young or too old for aerobic or anaerobic exercise. Increasing numbers of seniors, even into their eighties and nineties, are lifting weights and regaining strength that they thought had been lost forever. More and more runners in their fifties, sixties, seventies, and beyond are finishing 10Ks, half marathons, and even marathons. You'd be amazed at the limitless possibilities that await you, once you get started.

Different experts will offer different opinions, but there seems to be a great deal of support for the idea that one should complete fifteen to sixty minutes of aerobic exercise three to five days per week and do strength training—weightlifting and weight machines—on two more days. This combination of aerobic and anaerobic exercise will keep your body from becoming accustomed to doing one specific thing over and over. You'll work out different muscle groups on different days, and add to your body's overall health and well being.

Yoga and tai chi are also excellent ways to achieve balance, poise, strength, and endurance. Practically every yoga studio offers classes at the beginning level, which will be enough challenge for just about anyone. Even highly athletic folks find level two and level three yoga classes to be a demanding physical challenge. So don't overlook the martial arts and the gentle art of yoga when you are putting together your own fitness plan.

The fitness industry has never really figured out how to make itself attractive and appealing to older Americans. Go into most gyms, and the people you see are for the most part in their twenties and thirties, although depending on the community, you'll see older people as well. But not *that* many. That's why if you're going to join a gym—and I strongly recommend that you do—that you hire a trainer to work with you and offer you guidance as to what to do, how, and how often. Knowledge is power, especially on a weight room floor. You can also get into classes at a gym that will typically push you harder than you might have pushed yourself working out on your own. Many classes are right for newcomers to exercise and fitness; just ask a staff member which kind of class would make the most sense for you.

I understand that my older readers are going to find it harder to get into an exercise routine, for a lot of reasons. They might be telling themselves that they're too old, that their time has passed, that their body has slowed down, or any of a thousand other things. I want to urge you, if you are harboring any of those thoughts, to dismiss them. People a lot older than you are lifting weights, running, swimming, biking, doing triathlons, and pursuing other forms of physical fitness all the time. There's no such thing as too old! It is a fact that health clubs have not figured out how to make themselves attractive to older people. But look at it this way—you'll get to admire a lot of younger people as you are working out, and that's got to be worth something!

Regular exercise reduces your chances of both heart disease and osteoporosis. It gets your blood pressure into a healthy range—high blood pressure is a major source of discomfort at best and a killer at worst. Exercise reduces bad cholesterol and increases good cholesterol. It also reduces body fat. Obesity frequently leads to heart disease and diabetes; exercise, along with a good diet, is the key to reducing those risks. Exercise helps maintain healthy bone density, especially for older people, who are at risk of falling and breaking bones and suffering other injuries when their bones become brittle.

Exercise also builds strength, endurance, flexibility, and balance. As we age, we can lose a step. We experience loss of muscle, strength, and quality of tissue. Our aerobic fitness isn't the same. Joints stiffen, leading to a decreased range of motion and injuries. According to Joseph A. Buckwalter, M.D., more than 300,000 people a year break their hips due to falls. Exercise helps you keep your balance…it helps counter the effects of aging…and it makes you look good and feel good, too.

Exercise also has a powerful effect on mood disorders, including anxiety and depression. When you get your body moving, you get your mind moving, too. You just feel better. Whether a person is depressed on his own and lying on his own couch or a psychiatrist's couch, the right prescription doesn't always have to be something that comes in the form of a pill. Just getting up and moving—even something as simple as walking around the block—can have a salutary effect on our mood. The body was meant to move. It only makes sense that if the body goes motionless, the mind will become stagnant, as well.

Those are some of the many benefits that come from exercise. That's how your body and mind benefit, but what about your spirit? There's no doubt that your psyche and your self-esteem rise when you exercise. First, you're proud of yourself for taking time to get to the gym, get out for a walk or a bicycle ride, or getting to the pool for a swim. Second, you feel better. Third, you look in the mirror and you look better. And fourth, other people—family, friends, and even strangers—notice your healthy appearance, and it's always an ego boost to hear someone tell you how good you look! In short, there are a lot of great reasons for exercising and there aren't any good reasons for remaining stagnant or sedentary.

It's time to set aside any prejudices or negative feelings about exercise. The human body—*your* body—was meant to move. So get moving…to a gym, to a pool, or even around the block, and begin to enjoy the many health benefits that await you. The Bible speaks of Jacob's blessing—"long life, and length of days." It sounds redundant—why do you need long life *and* length of days? Exercise prolongs your life…and it gives you more energy to enjoy each and every day, with your children and grandchildren, at work, pursuing your hobbies and pastimes, doing whatever you love to do. Long life and length of days are yours for the taking. So go take them…and enjoy it!

Your health is your wealth—no matter how much money you have, you cannot buy your health back if you've lost it. You may gain it back slowly through some form of exercise, but you can't hire someone to exercise for you and expect the results to improve your body. The best exercise program is one that maintains good health for you. That requires consistency in everyday habits. Remember that good health is a habit and it takes twenty-one days to change or affirm a new habit. Once you establish this new habit don't break the cycle...or you'll revive your old habits and you'll have to start all over again. Set goals for yourself, live by the goals, and enjoy the results!

Part II:

Mind

Chapter 5

A Little Lower
Than the Angels

Animals run on instinct. The planets move in accordance with the laws of physics, the moon controls the tides, and tectonic plates govern the slow movement of the continents. Of all God's creations, only one possesses free will, consciousness, and the ability to discern right from wrong. That creature is man.

The human brain has been described as a "three pound universe" far more complex than any computer yet devised. The human mind can compose symphonies, write poetry, cure disease, and pray. The mind is an extraordinary gift, and yet, since we were equipped with it at birth, at no cost to us, we take it for granted, as we take practically everything that comes to us for no money down, no money later.

When the great motivator Zig Ziglar speaks, he says that he wishes he could sell everyone in the audience their brains for $100,000. That way, they would begin to place a value on their brains, and he would have $100,000 for everyone in the room! But $100,000 couldn't buy a new brain. No amount of money on earth could create a human mind. It's a gift from God, plain and simple.

The trouble comes when we misuse our mind, when we activate instinctual needs but we don't temper those needs and desires with balance, proportion, or a moral code. Criminologists have said that many lawbreakers believe that they have never done a wrong thing in their lives. The capacity of the human being to justify practically any form of bad behavior is boundless. Some people blame God for the ills of mankind—war, oppression, poverty, and the degradation of the environment. But when you really stop and think about it, and stopping and thinking is what this section of the book is all about, we can't blame God for these things. Man the creator, man the fixer, man the improver is all too often man the destroyer, leaving a trail of destruction, personal, political, and environmental, in his wake.

Doctors tell us that any medicine strong enough to help us is strong enough to hurt us, too. And so it is with the human mind—it's so powerful that it can build or destroy. The better use we make of our minds— the more attention we pay to their care and feeding—the happier we are as individuals, the better our relationships with our spouses and families, and the stronger our society and world become.

In the first section of the book, we saw that the Bible was God's diet and exercise manual, offering us clear and convincing guidance about how to nourish ourselves and how to take the best possible care of ourselves. Now we'll explore the question of what guidance the Bible gives us in terms of how to think. It's my contention that thinking is not just an automatic, reflex action. Instead, it's something that we can and must train ourselves to do in a way that maximizes the use of our God-given minds, so that we can live out God's expectation for us—that we become the best possible people we can be, and that our legacy to those around us is one of love, goodness, warmth, and support. As the legendary golfer Chi Chi Rodriguez likes to say, "What you take with you is what you leave behind."

The core of success in life is healthy thinking. Ralph Waldo Emerson wrote that there is really one mind, a universal Mind, the Mind of God, and each of our individual minds are inlets attached to a great ocean of thought. In other words, God directs our conscious thought, if we allow Him to do so, just as waves form in the ocean and push toward harbors and bays. The size of the waves can vary, depending on weather conditions, but the net effect is always the same—they bring great energy to bear on their ultimate destinations.

Another way to think about God is that He is the source of all power in the world, so that when we pray, talk to God, or otherwise connect with Him, by appreciating the beauty of a sunset or the smile of a child, we are experiencing true power. Everyone has a brain. We may not have the same intellect, and there are different types of intellects just as there are different learning styles. Our brains develop differently, based on the level of education we receive, but no one is using more than a small portion of his or her mental capacity. Again, we are the only creations endowed with consciousness. A chimpanzee can be taught to do basic math, but it cannot pass along its knowledge to a second chimpanzee. And as John Bradshaw, author and speaker on the subject of families, says, "Hyenas laugh, but they don't get the joke." Truly, we have been created a little lower than the angels, by virtue of the magnificent mind with which we have been endowed.

So the question arises: What's the proper use of the mind? Yes, human beings do have the ability to think great thoughts, compose symphonies, write sonnets, and design skyscrapers, but since only a few people can actually do those things, that cannot be the sole purpose of the thinking process. Instead, the most important thing we can do with our minds is develop our faith in God.

The Bible tells us that with God, all things are possible. And yet, we have no absolute, incontrovertible proof for the existence of God. If there were such proof, it would no longer require faith to believe in Him. And they don't call it a crawl of faith or a baby step of faith—they call it a leap of faith. So the question becomes, why should we make this leap of faith? What evidence can I offer for the assertion that the most important thing the human mind can do is develop a close relationship, a conscious contact, with God? And if that is all true, then how does one go about doing it?

As always, our starting point is the Bible. In both the Old and New Testaments, we see repeated examples of the blessings that flow when individuals devote their lives to faith. On a material level, the patriarchs of the Old Testament, Abraham, Isaac, and Jacob, were millionaires by our standards, commanding impressively large flocks of animals, owning broad masses of land, and spending their time with the kings, priests, and other temporal and religious leaders of their day. The Bible records that their lives constantly went better when they recognized God as the source of their life, success, and happiness.

When Moses led the Israelites out of Egypt across the divided Red Sea, he and his people turned back to see the entire Egyptian army, its vaunted military machine, drowned. The Israelites did not credit themselves with the occurrence of this saving miracle, of course. Instead, they sang a song of praise to God, who had made it happen, who had removed the slave people from the midst of the most powerful nation on earth by signs, wonders, and plagues heretofore unseen.

Shortly after their escape from Egypt, the forces of Amelek did battle with the Israelites. The Bible records that when Moses held his hands in the air, the Israelites prevailed on the battlefield; when he lowered his hands, the Amelekites would be vanquishing the Israelites. So Moses had his brother Aaron and another leader, Hur, assist him by holding his hands in the air. Bible scholars interpret the raised hands as a symbol of supplication of God's help, and the message that they draw from the story is that we prevail when we ask for God's help and we risk defeat when we do not.

Once the Israelites had made it safely to the desert, they received the Ten Commandments and dedicated themselves (when they were not bickering with their leader Moses) to building a tabernacle for the purpose of worshipping God. Much of the second half of the Book of Exodus is devoted to the details for the building of the tabernacle and the design of the vestments of the high priest who would enter in order to serve God. Much of the following Books of Leviticus and Numbers contain specifics about the animal offerings that were brought on the altar, first in the tabernacle in the desert and later in the great temple of Solomon erected in Jerusalem after the

Jews conquered the land. Again, the focus is not on what God can do for the Israelites but on how the Israelites were to serve God.

The lesson of the Old Testament is clear: Our modern approach to religion has things backwards. The first question is not what God can do for us. The first question is what we can do for God. The Israelites spent forty years of wandering in the desert in an effort to learn how best to serve God, mentally, through prayer, and physically, through the daily service in the tabernacle. The reward for this service was the privilege of entering, conquering, and settling the Holy Land, which remained under the Israelites' dominion, with just one interruption, for more than a thousand years. The purpose of the mind, the Old Testament teaches, is to develop faith and to serve God.

In the New Testament, the lesson is the same: Faith in God is the ultimate purpose of man. Jesus viewed with grave alarm the corruption among the Pharisees who controlled worship in the temple, and he and his disciples were essentially a renegade band of brothers committed to bringing people back to God. [Examples?] His message, while well received among individuals, flew in the face of the political leaders of the day, who rightly recognized that if power were lodged with God, then the power of individual political leaders would be diminished. So the campaign against Jesus that led ultimately to His crucifixion rightly can be viewed as a power struggle between those who would have people place their primary reliance on God and those who sought to keep that power for themselves, and we all know how that story ended.

The lesson, once again, is clear—the purpose of the human being is not to glorify himself but instead to consider the greatness of God and to feel both reverential awe and fatherly love. The parables of the Bible reinforce the idea that the most important thing we can do is turn our minds to God. One of the best-known and best-loved parables of the New Testament is that of the prodigal son who burns through his inheritance, lives a dissipated lifestyle, and yet is welcomed with open arms by his father upon his return. So it is with us—many of us are tempted by our popular culture which stresses the ego and the satisfaction of pleasureful desire over and above an idea of God-consciousness. But when we return our thoughts to God, He always welcomes us back with open arms.

Many people ask how faith can be possible in our world, where the newspapers are full of stories of war, crime, and suffering. I'm certainly not here to minimize or downplay the suffering that people experience, but I am here to say that God, in His own words in the Bible, told us that we have free choice. Ninety-five percent of the pain and suffering in this world was not inflicted by God on people. Instead, it is the outgrowth of choices that people make. In the Bible, God might have directed one nation to make war against others. But in today's world, contrary to what some may claim, God makes no such demands. People choose to make war. People choose to commit crime. People choose to misuse their free will and hurt one another in a myriad of ways. Is it fair to blame God for the choices that people make?

Although God has the capacity to make every decision for us, so that we only make good choices, He has obviously chosen not to do that. He has given us a free will to make choices and the choices we make decide our fate. If you base your life's choices on what you want, what you desire and what makes you feel good, then how can you blame God for the outcome? We all have choices and each chapter of our life is determined on the choices we make.

The Psalmist tells us that God's thoughts are not like our thoughts, which means that we human beings simply do not have the mental capacity to understand why God created the world, or why God created people with free will and therefore with the ability to do terrible things to one another. But the existence of war, crime, or human cruelty in general does not disprove the existence of God. Instead, it shows that when God said that He was giving human beings free will, He wasn't kidding.

If ninety-five percent of the pain and suffering in the world is in fact a reflection of the choices that people make to cause each other harm, then the remaining five percent could rightly be called tragedy. No human being could possibly explain the existence of tragedy, other than to understand it as a teacher, and to help us. The main lesson of tragedy is to teach us to value every day with those we love, because we truly never know what tomorrow may bring. Should the existence of tragedy cause one to deny the existence of God? Absolutely not. It's not something that we can understand, but there are few things we completely understand and yet we can benefit from them—everything from the power of love to warm our hearts to the power of electricity to warm our homes. We don't have to fully understand something in order for us to benefit from it or feel grateful for it.

The next thing to consider is the question of whether God exists at all, or whether we humans invented a God concept, or many different God concepts, in order to assuage our fears, explain the inexplicable, and otherwise just get us through the night. Well, let's look at the evidence. What are the chances that the universe as we know it could have arisen on its own? What are the chances that the laws of physics that explain the orbits of planets, the movement of the waves, the rising and setting of the sun, the changing of the seasons, could simply be something set in motion at random? What are the odds that nature essentially could have created itself, from a single-celled organism to the astonishing variety of fish in the sea, birds in the sky, animals on the ground, and then the pinnacle of creation, man himself (or herself)? Indeed, scientists have pondered this very question and have concluded that the possibility that the universe lacks a Creator has approximately the same odds as an individual reaching into a bowl containing eighty-two billion red balls and one black ball…and picking out the black ball on the very first try. When you stop and think about it, it makes no sense that the world could have created itself or otherwise evolved into the world as we know it.

Think about the magnificence that is the human body. Consider all the various functions that the human body can perform, in one neat, not so little package. We can experience the world through our five senses, we can bend the physical world to our purposes, and we can use our minds to contemplate our own purpose and the existence of God. We really are pretty remarkable! How did we get here? How did *anything* get here? As the expression goes, the believer only has to explain the existence of God. The atheist has to explain everything else.

So if the Bible teaches us that faith in God is the appropriate response of the human being to His existence, how, then, are we expected to find our way to faith?

The first thing we have to do is ask ourselves what blocks or impediments exist in our own minds keeping us from faith. First, it can be just plain hard to concentrate on the idea of God, given the increasing number of distractions we face in our daily lives. Millennia ago, the personalities of the Bible did not have television, Internet, radio, cell phones, or PDAs to distract them. They lived in nature, not divorced from it. They could not be workaholics, for the simple reason that once darkness fell, work ceased. It has been said that we moderns work harder than did the slaves in Egypt. We certainly work more hours than they did! So the first thing we have to do is turn off the distractions—get away from the e-mail, step away from the computer screen, and take a moment to concentrate our minds on the idea that God exists, that He cares about us, that He truly is our Father in Heaven. Even an act as simple as taking a walk in nature (while leaving all our pocket-held devices either in the car or in off-mode) can help us make this happen.

We then must undertake a thorough examination of our ideas about God. Not all of us came out of our childhood homes equipped with a concept of God as loving and caring. All too many Christians received in their churches and families a concept of an angry, distant, punishing God. Who would want to have a relationship with a Being like that? So if we are going to give the God concept a fair shake, it's up to each of us to examine what prejudices we might have about God and ask ourselves whether it is appropriate, at this point in our spiritual development, to jettison them in favor of a more loving concept of a Creator.

If you have children, you love them no matter what they do. That's how God feels about us, plain and simple. Why is it essential to recognize this truth? It all comes back to the initial topic of this chapter—that the most important use of the mind is to "plug in" to the ultimate power source in the world, which is God. If we keep to dysfunctional concepts of God that we might have developed earlier in our lives, we will never be able to avail ourselves fully of the power that God offers.

What can this power do? The individual who feels a loving connection with God is far more likely to be an emotionally strong and satisfied person. I'm not saying there aren't happy atheists out there! I am saying that individuals who do feel a connection with their Creator are more often than not content with themselves although constantly striving to be more, and do more, and accomplish more. As a result, they tend to make more successful members of families. Their marriages are stronger. They are often more successful in their careers, and because they see life as something more than self-gratification, they tend to make greater contributions of their time, abilities, and financial resources to their community and their society. They know who they are and they know where they're going. They don't feel the impossible burden to figure everything out on their own, because they understand that the basic questions are beyond our understanding—how the world got here, where everything is headed. They find answers to these questions in Bible study and in close communion with God, and as a result, they live more centered lives.

How do you develop a healthy, satisfying relationship with God? By turning your mind to thoughts of God. This can be done through formal prayer or even just informal "conversations with God." Certainly God can be found in the church sanctuary, but He can also be found on the factory floor, in the office building, in the car, in the home, wherever you are. When people say they feel distant from God, the obvious question arises: "Who moved?"

If we want any relationship to succeed, we have to put the time in. And so it is when trying to create or enhance a relationship with God. This doesn't mean that we have to go off to seminary for two years, although there's nothing wrong with that! It does mean that we need to strive for consistency by praying every day, by incorporating religious services into our lives, by making time for study, and then by putting into practice what we have learned. The Bible tells us that faith without works is dead, so a live faith requires a constant demonstration of our faith. This isn't as hard as it sounds—if we are acting out of love and service to our fellows, that's all God asks.

In sum, the human mind is indeed capable of creating and accomplishing all sorts of other great things. But the primary purpose of the mind is to connect with God, to plug into the ultimate Source of all power. When we do so, we are preparing ourselves to meet our primary responsibility on earth, to love God and serve people, to love people and serve God. That's the real purpose of the mind. Many people don't recognize that the mind is like a muscle—it can be exercised and strengthened. How to strengthen the mind is the subject of the next chapter.

Chapter 6

Exercising Your Mind

Everybody knows you can exercise your body. You can go to the gym, you can go for a walk or a run, and you can swim or ride a bike. Through diet and exercise, as we saw in the first section of this book, we can reshape our bodies and increase our level of health, fitness, and energy. Most people don't realize, however, that they can exercise their minds and get equally awesome and exciting results.

North America in the late eighteenth century. We've all heard estimates that we use only three to ten percent of the power of our minds. Nightingale says that the American continent, in the late eighteenth century, was settled, and only sporadically, along its eastern shore, alongside the Atlantic Ocean. The rest of the continent, all of its riches, lay untapped; waiting for explorers to discover the richness it held. Nightingale says that our minds are equally undeveloped—so the question arises, how can we make use of the ninety to ninety-five percent of our capacity for thought that has previously gone untapped?

Before we can figure out how best to use our minds, we have to understand what our minds are. In 1960, in his groundbreaking work Psycho-Cybernetics, Maxwell Maltz wrote that the brain is a computer—and not just any computer, but a question-answering computer. In other words, if you ask yourself a question, your brain will think and think and think until it comes up with an appropriate answer. So the quality of the output of our brains—the answers to the questions it generates—is in direct correlation with the quality of the questions we ask ourselves. If we want our brains to generate great answers, if we want to develop our ability to generate ideas, the first thing to do is to recognize that we must ask ourselves better questions.

Anthony Robbins, perhaps the leading motivator of our day, takes this a step further. Robbins says that if we ask ourselves, "Why do I always mess up my [fill in the blank—relationships, jobs, whatever]?" the brain will work overtime trying to generate an answer, and the answer won't be a positive one. It will be something along the lines of, "Because I'm an idiot!" And that's as far as most people take things—they fail at things, they make mistakes, and they erroneously conclude that since they've made mistakes, they cannot be very intelligent. Smart people, after all, don't make mistakes, do they?

Of course they do! Smart people get it wrong all the time! The classic examples are the Hall of Fame baseball player who makes an out seven out of ten times...but still has a .300 batting average. Or Thomas Edison, who attempted thousands of different experiments before he was able to create a working light bulb. Legendary UCLA basketball coach John Wooden would say that "The team that makes the most mistakes wins." And as the expression goes, "Show me a man who hasn't made mistakes and I'll show you a man who hasn't made anything."

In other words, successful people don't necessarily expect them to get everything right the first time. They know that success is a process not of perfectionism but of repeated, sustained effort over a long period of time. So when people make mistakes and therefore conclude that they are never going to succeed, they're right! They're *not* going to succeed, because they have essentially told themselves that they won't...and we believe pretty much everything we tell ourselves.

So the first thing we have to do, if we are to develop our minds, is to ask ourselves better questions...and to stop being satisfied with answers that paint us as stupid, or failures, or anything negative. After all, we are reflections of our Creator, and God does not create junk! The only person who can really convince us that we will never amount to anything is the man or woman in the mirror. And the way we get out of that mindset of negativity is to ask better questions.

Robbins says that the antidote to asking, "Why do I always mess things up?" is this: "How can I succeed in the area of [romance, finance, work, whatever]…and have a great time while I'm doing it?" You can easily see that the human brain, a question answering device, is far more likely to come up with positive ideas when asked a question like that than when confronted with the concept of, "Why am I such a loser?" If you want better results in your life, if you want to use your mind more effectively, start by asking better questions.

We saw in the previous chapter that the ultimate purpose of the mind is to connect us with God. But that's not the only thing the mind does. It also generates ideas about every aspect of our lives, from how we live to how we work, from relationships with people to the relationship we have with ourselves. The individuals in our society who are compensated the most, who find themselves lionized in the media, and who achieve astonishing fame and success, are the people who generate—and then put into practice—the best ideas. Bill Gates is one of the wealthiest men in the world not because he is handsome or strong (although when he stands on his bankbook, he sure is tall!). It's because he had an idea—put a computer on every person's desk—and he worked to make that idea a reality. Warren Buffett is one of the world's most successful investors not because he spends his days printing newspaper, making chocolates, or selling fractional shares of jets. Instead, he had the wisdom and foresight to invest in companies that did these things, and he and his investors have reaped massive rewards. Buffett is successful because of the ideas he generated…and because of the effort he made putting them into practice.

And so it is with every successful person in our society. Hard work is an absolute necessity and prerequisite for success, but we all know countless numbers of people who have worked hard all their lives and don't have the smallest fraction of the wealth of a Gates or a Buffett to show for it. So hard work is important, but it's not everything. The most important thing is the ability to generate brilliant ideas and then act on them appropriately.

Can we train our minds to develop ideas? Absolutely! Earl Nightingale offers an intriguing suggestion. He says that since the mind is like a muscle, it needs to be exercised. Since the purpose of the mind is to generate ideas (or to receive ideas from a divine source), we need to practice the concept of idea generation on a daily basis. Nightingale offers a simple method for doing so. Every morning, he says, along with your cup of coffee, sit down with a yellow pad and a pen. Pose yourself a question or a problem that needs attention, either in your workplace or your personal life, and then come up with twenty different ideas for solving that problem. Don't stop until you've come up with twenty solutions. Nightingale says that most people tend to think of a problem, come up with one solution, and then act on that solution. By doing so, they may be acting out of fear, greed, or some other negative human emotion. The wiser course is to stop and look for alternatives to that first idea—nineteen alternatives, to be exact! Nightingale tells us that many of the ideas will be no good at all, and that coming up with ideas eighteen, nineteen, and twenty, at least at first, may feel like pulling teeth. But if we are thorough about this process, and keep at it, we will discover, to our surprise and delight, that we are indeed capable of generating some amazing ideas to problems—ideas that we would never have thought of had we not taken the time to explore the virgin territory that is the ninety to ninety-five percent of our minds that we typically never use.

Try this idea generation technique tomorrow morning with your first cup of coffee, and don't get up until you've generated all twenty ideas! See how far your mind can take you. Nightingale points out that if a person practices this technique five days a week, that adds up to a hundred new ideas a week, four hundred new ideas a month, and more than five thousand ideas a year. What would your career, financial life, or personal life look like if you developed a reputation for generating five thousand new ideas every year? Chances are that your life would absolutely explode if you were to try this approach. I hope you will!

Now that we know how to exercise our minds, let's turn to the idea of the relationship between our conscious and subconscious minds. I'm not going to get into complex scientific analyses of the way the mind works, but it's important to have a general understanding. To keep it simple and clear, remember this one fact: your subconscious mind believes everything you say. If you tell yourself that you're smart, your mind will believe you. If you tell yourself that you're stupid or weak and that nothing ever works out, your mind will believe you. The subconscious mind cannot distinguish between reality and whatever you say is reality. Twenty years ago, a small earthquake in northern Italy, a region not known for earthquakes, destroyed a few buildings and caused structural damage to many more, but caused practically no injuries. Two people died of heart attacks nevertheless. Were they or their homes threatened by the earthquake? No. But they believed they were going to die, and they did. Such is the power of the mind—it can convince us that all is lost. If we were not capable of feeling that way, there would be no suicides. We only give up when we are devoid of hope. We lose hope only when we have convinced ourselves that nothing good can happen. And yet, as we have seen, every successful person has been through failure, often multiple and heartbreaking failures. The ability to bounce back is not an aspect of our physical beings—it's an aspect of our minds. We need mental resiliency as much as we need physical resiliency if we are to survive and succeed in this world.

Since your subconscious mind, which represents ninety-five percent of your thinking, believes every single word that your conscious mind tells it, the obvious result is that we must always tell our minds positive things about ourselves. We can't tell ourselves outright falsehoods, but we can shape the truths about ourselves in ways that support our growth instead of hindering it. We all know that if we tell a child repeatedly that he is not smart, that he is not capable of learning, that he's destined to fail, the child will believe that fact. We forget that if we adults tell ourselves the same things, we are dooming ourselves to failure. So you have to make it completely unacceptable to tell yourself anything negative about yourself. First of all, we have all been created in God's divine image—so when we are telling ourselves that we have little or no value, we are actually devaluing God. But even if we remove the spiritual aspect from this discussion, it makes obvious sense that we have to saturate our minds with positive thinking—not impossible or implausible thinking, but positive thinking about ourselves. Otherwise, we are creating a mental obstacle too great to be overcome.

Sometimes people fear that because they have spent their whole lives thinking negatively, they won't be able to make the switch to positive thinking. Well, that's just more negative thinking, isn't it? Of course it is! So the question becomes, how do you flip a switch from negative to positive? One approach is to listen carefully to the way you talk to yourself. One exercise that many people have found extremely educational is to keep a notebook with you for an entire day and write down *every single word you tell yourself.* Whatever you say, positive or negative, goes into the notebook. Then, at the end of the day, take a look at what you wrote. What was the balance between positive and negative? In what ways did you enhance your self-image, and in what ways did you cut yourself down? Take a closer look at the negative things you said. Would you allow anyone else to say these things to you about you to your face? Would you permit anyone else to say things like that about your spouse, or your children? Absolutely not. You wouldn't permit others to talk about you this way, so why do you give yourself permission to run yourself down in this manner?

The simple answer is that we do so without being aware of what we are saying or doing. If we knew better, we would do better! Well, if you complete that exercise, and I hope you will, you'll discover the precise language that you use in order to beat yourself up. How do you stop talking to yourself that way? Here's the answer: From now on, every time you hear yourself saying the slightest negative thing about yourself, ranging from critical or self-deprecating comments all the way to the use of expletives on yourself, say, *out loud,* "Thank you for sharing, but I would rather not be addressed in that manner!"

It sounds silly, but saying those exact words, out loud—"Thank you for sharing, but I would rather not be addressed in that manner!"—makes all the difference. It takes twenty-one days to create and lock in a new habit. Over the next twenty-one days, you will be destroying the habit of destroying yourself. It typically takes people twenty or thirty times saying, "Thank you for sharing, but…" out loud, before negative self-talk dwindles away to nothing, or next to nothing. One of the worst things about self-criticism is that it puts us in an unhappy state, and then we tend to take out our unhappiness on the people around us, often the people closest to us, like family members or coworkers (or even the boss!). The great thing about positive self-talk—and about interrupting our negative self-talk patterns with that magical phrase, is that it actually makes us laugh! It's really hard to say, "Thank you for sharing, but I would rather not be addressed in that manner!" without laughing, or at least smiling a little bit. That laughter will instantly change your mental state from negative to positive. And you will wipe away one of the most destructive habits that many human beings—perhaps most human beings— possess—sabotaging ourselves verbally. Now you are telling your mind that you are not to be spoken to in this negative way. If no one else has permission to address you harshly, why should you have the right to do so? Again, you are a beautiful child of God, not some automaton or piece of junk. You deserve the best. We can't expect the best from others until we are willing and capable to treat ourselves well first.

We have seen that the mind can be developed like a muscle, and we've also seen that we subconsciously use our minds as weapons against ourselves, until we learn to stop. We touched briefly a moment ago on the subject of mental states. Let's take a deeper look at this critically important point as a means of rounding out our discussion on how to exercise the mind.

What do people want? What do you want? Most people want to be reasonably successful, reasonably happy, reasonably wealthy, and comfortable within themselves. So we devote enormous efforts to the activities that we think will generate these mental states. In so doing, however, many of us take on behaviors and attitudes that actually drive us further away from those desired mental states instead of closer to them. We decide that we want to make a million dollars so that we can take better care of our loved ones, but we end up spending all our time at work and thus we destroy our relationships at home. Or we neglect our physical bodies in the quest to make careers and names for ourselves. As the expression goes, we spend our health to gain wealth, and then we spend our wealth to regain our health. Not a winning ticket! Is there an alternative?

There is. And that is to distinguish, as Anthony Robbins teaches, between what he calls "end goals" and "means goals." Robbins says that people tell him, "I want to make a lot of money." Or "I want to have a great relationship." And Robbins says he always asks the simple question, "Why?"

The question often takes people by surprise. "Why?" they repeat, somewhat incredulous that Robbins wouldn't know the answer. "Because I want to be happy!"

"Well," Robbins replies, "what if you could be happy right now?"

Typically, people have no idea what he's talking about! So he elaborates: What we really seek in life are mental states—happiness, security, and above all, peace of mind. But instead of focusing on those mental states, which really are what we desire, we spend all our time focusing on the means by which we think we will attain those mental states. We think that if we have a million dollars in the bank, we'll feel better about our lives. Or we think that if we have a great relationship, we'll feel happier with ourselves. What Robbins is saying is that instead of concentrating on what we want to achieve, we spend all our time concentrating on something we think will give us those goals. Why not skip all the work of trying to accomplish all those "means goals"—the million dollars in the bank, the great relationship—and instead aim directly for the "ends goals"—the mental states of happiness, success, and peace of mind, that we really crave?

"How would you feel right now," Robbins asks, "if you had a million dollars in the bank?"

Typically, the person responds, "Wow! I would feel great!"

Robbins goes further. "How would you stand? How would you walk around? How would you smile? How much more generous would you feel toward other people?" The answer of course, is that we would stand taller, be more relaxed, breathe more deeply, feel more generous and compassionate toward others, and so on. In other words, we can access immediately the end state of peace of mind without going to all the trouble of making the million dollars! And when we do feel relaxed, more connected with ourselves and with the world, more open to new ideas, and more generous and compassionate to the rest of the world, it stands to reason that whatever we want to accomplish, from creating a great relationship to putting a million dollars in the bank, is going to be a million times easier.

The trick in life, therefore, is to stop focusing on the means goals and instead define clearly for ourselves our ends goals—what we really want. There are far too many stories of individuals who had millions in the bank and ended their own lives because they were so unhappy. Most people take the wrong lesson from these cautionary tales. Most people interpret these stories to mean that having money makes you unhappy. As the expression goes, I've been broke and I've been rich, and rich is better! Money isn't everything, but it is indeed important. The focusing on the means goal of "making a million dollars" when it's really the end goal that we desire—"peace of mind"—is backwards thinking, and yet it's the way that practically all of us tend to think. If we knew better, we would do better. Now you know better!

It's vitally important to set goals, and in the next chapter, one of the things we will discuss is how to turn the goal-setting process to your advantage. But in the meantime, it's important to remember what our real goals in life are. For most of us, they start with peace of mind, health, move on to having great relationships with ourselves, with God, and with those around us, and then include financial success and career advancement. We can access the emotional states we desire at any time, simply by standing taller, breathing more deeply, and acting as if we have already achieved our means goals. And in so doing, we make our means goals—the money in the bank, the great relationship, and the great job, the improvement in our health—immeasurably easier to attain.

We can use our minds as weapons with which to cut ourselves down, or we can use them as the foundation for a life of true success—spiritual meaning, love and connection, achievement, and financial success. You've now got your mental exercise program. Start generating twenty new ideas a day. Speak to yourself only in a positive manner, because God doesn't have grandchildren! And remember what your real goals are—the mental states that you can access this very second. God gave you a mind for a purpose, and with these tools, you can begin to access the undeveloped terrain in the most important real estate of all—the space between your ears. So go to it!

So far we've seen how you can improve your health and your mind by following the guidance in the Bible and strengthening your faith in God. But these blessings aren't all He wants you to enjoy! Next let's take a look at something I know all of us have thought of in the past—money—and learn how God can help you enjoy prosperity and abundance in your life as well as health.

Chapter 7

Does God Want You To Be Rich? Yes!

Answer the following question with the first word that comes to mind. No thinking, no pondering, no looking for the "right answer." Ready? Here goes:

"Rich people are…."

What did you put down? If you're like most people, the first thought that came to mind was negative. Most of us tend to think that wealthy people are mean, selfish, self-centered, greedy, hypocritical, or just downright evil. The reality is, more often than not, the opposite. Pound for pound, wealthy people are more generous than the poor, simply because they can afford to be more generous. They've got the resources to help others not just with their time but with their money, and many have a well-honed sense of the need to give back. It was true more than a century ago when Andrew Carnegie made dozens of his employee's millionaires and endowed educational institutions and libraries across the country. It's just as true today, when Bill Gates' foundation is committed to spending billions of dollars to make one billion people across the world who could not otherwise afford access to computers, computer literate. The importance of giving back goes back a long way, to the time of the Old Testament, when Jacob promised to give God one-tenth of all that he earned.

Are there wealthy people who are greedy, selfish, lazy, indifferent, or downright evil? Of course there are. The rich are no different from the rest of us in the sense that there is a broad range of personality types among them, and indeed, we cannot use every wealthy person as a role model in life. There are two lessons to be learned from the foregoing. First, wealthy people are often far more generous than the rest of us realize. And second, many people who desire wealth actually erect an impenetrable mental roadblock by believing that the rich are bad or evil. If we don't want to think of ourselves as evil, we will do whatever it takes to keep us from that state. And if wealthy people are evil, then it stands to reason that we will do everything we can to keep ourselves from getting rich!

It's crazy, but indeed that logic dictates how many of us think, and act, when it comes to money. Many of us misunderstand the Biblical admonition that "money is the root of all evil." The actual language of the Bible tell us that "*love* of money is the root of all evil," and what it really means is that placing the love of money above all other things in life is the source of trouble, disharmony, and unhappiness. Money is nothing more than a medium of exchange. It is a way of exchanging value, so that people can benefit from the labor of others. Money is not something to be shunned. It doesn't make bad people good or good people bad. It's something that exists in the world, and we need to have a healthy relationship with it if we are to enjoy the kind of financial success that God wants us to have and that we need if we are to make our way in today's expensive world.

In their book *Why We Want You To Be Rich*, Donald Trump and Robert Kiyosaki make the point that we can no longer rely on the government or employers to ensure our financial stability or even our survival. Trump and Kiyosaki want the rest of us to be rich, because when we are financially capable of controlling our destinies, then we, the people, will increase our power. If we fail to do so, then government and business will claim even more power, thus further diminishing the importance and the security of the individual. They want us to be rich in order to create a bulwark against encroaching governmental and business power.

I want you to be rich for a different reason—I want you to be rich because God wants you to be rich. God has created a world of astonishing abundance. We who were blessed to live in the United States of America, the freest society the world has ever known, have an overabundance of material goods, food and drink, clothing, vehicles, homes, and "toys" from which to choose. The average middle class American residing in a 1500 square foot home lives far more opulently and with more creature comforts than any king or emperor, up to the dawn of the twentieth century, could ever have imagined. The whole world is literally at our feet. The role models of the Bible were wealthy. There is nothing ennobling to the human soul about poverty or degradation. I'm not talking about piling up material goods so that we can compete with the Joneses down the block. I am talking about the fact that God created an abundant universe, and he wants us, as his children, to benefit and to enjoy ourselves and our lives richly.

So the first thing we have to do is scrub our minds of any negativity that we may have toward money. And that makes this an appropriate time to introduce the concept of scarcity versus abundance thinking. There are two ways to think about money and about life. One is rooted in scarcity—a sense that there isn't enough to go around. Enough what? Enough of anything. Enough money, enough time, enough food, enough clothing, enough medicine, enough of whatever it is that we think we need in order to be happy. Scarcity thinking is marked by statements like "Money doesn't grow on trees!" Or "You better save it for a rainy day." The underlying message of those statements is that there isn't enough, and you better conserve or even hoard what you have, because trouble not only can come but will come, and you've got to be ready.

Does this kind of thinking sound even remotely spiritual? Is it possible to reconcile such a negative outlook on life with the abundance we see in nature? How do we square this kind of "poverty thinking" with the lush lifestyles of the Biblical patriarchs, whom God surely intended as role models for mankind throughout time? The simple answer is that we cannot. God wants us to be successful, happy, and secure—secure in our knowledge of His love for us and secure in the material blessings He wants to bestow upon us so that we can maximize our enjoyment of life and at the same time give to others less fortunate than ourselves. We saw in the previous chapter that our subconscious minds, which represent ninety-five percent of our thinking capacity, believe whatever we say. So the starting point on the road to becoming financially secure is to examine our minds for any thoughts rooted in poverty thinking, which is also called "coming from lack," and then root those thoughts out without mercy. It is simply impossible to develop a financial successful life on a foundation of negative thinking.

I asked you at the outset of this chapter to give your "first gut" response to the question of how you feel about wealthy people. Take a second look at the answer that you gave. Was it rooted in envy? Jealousy? Negativity? If so, where did those beliefs come from? Were they implanted in you by a parent? By a teacher? By a well meaning but errant religious leader in your childhood or youth? Or did it come from the popular media? Popular culture is all about tearing down wealthy and successful people, so as to play to the more base aspects of human nature rooted in negativity, jealousy, and envy. In the previous chapter, we talked about the importance of identifying and stopping negative self-talk, in order to create peace of mind. Now, we need to identify and eliminate any negative thoughts we might have about money or about people who have money, so that we can begin to build a new and solid foundation for our financial futures.

The opposite of poverty thinking is prosperity thinking or "coming from abundance." Prosperity thinking tells us that there is enough—in fact, there's more than enough. There's enough for us and there's more than enough to go around. Prosperity thinking doesn't mean we can sit on our duffs and wait for money to rain down from the heavens. We have to take action and more action. We have to develop thinking patterns that generate great ideas, as we saw in the last chapter. And then we have to work at making our dreams come true. But the "work" necessary in order to achieve prosperity isn't always the kind of "nose to the grindstone," eighty-hour workweek kind of toil we think is necessary. Some of the wealthiest people in the world devote a remarkably small portion of their day to their working lives. How do they do it? And how can you use your own mind to create abundance and prosperity in your life?

To make the move from scarcity thinking to abundance or prosperity thinking, we've seen that the first step is to eliminate negative attitudes about money that we may possess. Again, it's impossible to bring more money into our lives if we have negative attitudes toward money or to those who have more money. And then the question becomes how we go about creating a mindset that invites prosperity. It all starts with written goals.

We saw in the previous chapter that the mind is a question-answering machine. Our Creator also constructed our minds to be goal-oriented as well. Human beings need worthy goals in order to feel good about themselves, to feel motivated, and even simply to get out of bed in the morning. Steven H. Morton, author of *Ten Common Mistakes Retirees Make*, writes that the year after retirement is all too often marked by the "three D's"—depression, divorce, and even death. That's because when we're working, we have goals in mind, whether they are specific or vague, written or just carried in our brains. For many people, when they stop working, they lose the motivation to carry on with their lives, so much so that they are unable or unwilling to face the reality that their identity has changed. They have much more time to spend with their spouse, and their entire life is something new and even bewildering, since it no longer revolves around work. This is an excellent illustration of the fact that when we don't have goals, we founder. We're at sea. We don't get where we want to go, because we don't know where we want to go.

When we set goals for ourselves, we are taking the time to commit to a course of action that will lead to desirable outcomes that we believe will improve our lives. We were constructed to live our lives in pursuit of worthy goals, and we will be rewarded. As the Book of Deuteronomy says, "…these blessings shall come upon you and overtake you, because you obey the voice of the Lord your God." So how do we choose worthy goals for ourselves?

One approach is to look at our lives as having different components. There's a spiritual side of life, and we can call that Faith. There is Finance. There's Fitness. There's Family. There's Fun. Take a look at each of these words, which conveniently begin with the letter F, for ease of use, and ask yourself this: One year from today, where would you like to be in each of these categories?

With regards to Faith, where would you like to be on your walk? What do you want your relationship with God to look like a year from today? Don't worry about how you're going to get there. And don't make the goal so impossibly high that no human being could attain it. "I want to comprehend God in all His totality" might be a little much—especially for one year! A more appropriate goal for a human being in this area might be, "I have a strong faith in God and I pray and meditate daily."

Let's move on to Finance. How much money would you like to have in the bank a year from now? How much money would you like to earn over the next twelve months? Write the numbers down—those are your financial goals.

What about Fitness? Is there a certain amount of weight that you might want to drop? What do you want your body to look like a year from now? And so on down the line, with each of these categories. The result will be that you have specific goals in each of the important departments of your life. If there's another area of your life that isn't on this list, by all means add it, because this is all about you and your goals. I'm simply presenting the areas of life to which most people can relate.

What do you do with your goals? Copy them onto an index card and keep them in your wallet and purse. Some experts suggest that you should review your goals first thing in the morning and then just before you go to sleep, so as to saturate your mind with the destination that you are creating. Keep in mind as you write your goals down on that index card that your subconscious mind doesn't understand the idea of past, present, or future. If you want to make your goal real to your subconscious mind, just write down the goal as if it is already happening in the present moment. For example, "I earn $100,000 a year"—not "I will earn $100,000 per year." If you tell your subconscious mind that you "will" do something, then it says, "It's not happening now, so I don't have to be concerned with it." Such statements aren't really goals—they're more in the line of aspirations, hopes, or wishes. When we express goals in a concrete way and in the present tense, they become real to our subconscious. "I weigh 170 pounds and have fifteen percent body fat" is a clear, concise goal that your subconscious mind can understand. That's a lot more effective than saying; "I lost some weight this year." What is your subconscious mind supposed to do with a statement like that? If you put down on your goal card "I have an outstanding marriage," that's a much better way of describing what you want than saying, "My wife and I didn't fight as much this year." You see where I'm going here—make your goals clear and concise, put them in the present tense, and then watch what happens.

As long as you've got written goals, your subconscious mind will seek to make those goals a reality. The subconscious hates the confusion or dissonance created by hearing one thing and knowing that it isn't true yet. So the subconscious mind will do everything it can to make your goal true. In a concrete sense, you will become more attuned to opportunities to reach your goals—a posting for a job that will allow you to reach your financial goal, a magazine article or book that will help you improve your relationship, an approach to diet and exercise that will help you eliminate those unwanted pounds. On a spiritual level, goals are messages we send out into the universe about who we want to be. The universe typically rewards those who use the mechanism of goal-setting by bringing down opportunities, connections, coincidences, synchronicities—whatever you want to call them—that seemingly come from nowhere but bring us to the realization of our goals.

How powerful are written goals? Motivational speakers often quote a survey of Yale University graduates from the early 1960s. It turns out that the three percent of the class who had written goals enjoyed a combined net worth greater than the remaining ninety-seven percent of their classmates. This is an astonishing figure, and the truth of it has been borne out by study after study. People who have goals—and especially people who have written goals—unlock the key to power in the universe and, as the New Testament says, "Mighty forces will come to your aid." Goal setting triggers those mighty forces within us and around us to help us make our dreams come true.

We've talked about eliminating poverty thinking, uprooting within us any negativity we might have toward wealthy people or money in general, and we've talked about the power of setting goals. Now let's go more deeply into the question of what prosperity thinking is all about and how to attain it. In order to do so, I want to introduce you to a new way to think about the power of the mind. Most of us think of the mind as an idea-generating computer, and that has certainly been our focus up to this point. The mind actually has another vital purpose, one that many people frequently overlook. And here we begin to get into a more spiritual or even metaphysical approach to thinking, so stay with me if the ideas seem new or strange.

I want you to begin to think of the mind as a receiving station for ideas, not just a generator of ideas. We spoke earlier of the concept of the universal mind—that each of our individual minds are inlets within the great ocean of thought that has its roots in the divine. When you put thoughts "out there" into the universe, like a message in a bottle, amazing things happen. And the most powerful way to direct your thoughts so that you can begin to reap the prosperity that God has in store for you is by the practice of affirmations. The meaning of the word affirmation is contained within the word itself—the word "firm." Affirmations are a way of making firm, clear, and plain to ourselves and to the listening universe exactly what we desire in life. The practice of affirmations is entirely spiritual when we use it for good ends, and is entirely compatible with Christian thought. Affirmations are a sort of offshoot of goal setting. We have seen that negative affirmations have huge power over us.

In the previous chapter, we talked about how negative thinking can destroy any possibility of a positive self-image. Now we want to see the other side of the coin—we want to see how positive thinking and especially constructive thinking through the use of affirmations can bring about a change inside ourselves and in our world. An affirmation is a positive statement put in the present tense that expresses what you would like to happen by describing it as your current reality. Not "I would like to lose thirty pounds" but "I am at my ideal weight." Not "I need to make more money" but "I earn $100,000 a year." How are these different from goals? It's best to have a relatively small number of overall goals—say, four to six, one for each important department of your life. Anything more than that and we don't really know what goal to pursue first. With affirmations, you can create as many as you want and you can repeat them as often as you want. When you write yourself a set of affirmations, each one beginning "I am" and then continuing with a description of how you want things to be, you are in effect creating new software for the operating system that is your brain. Instead of operating on vague wishes and hopes, your brain now has the power to act on the specific, clear-cut desires that you are making firm through your words.

What's so spiritual about affirmations? Think about how God created the world! According to the Book of Genesis, He didn't create the universe with a backhoe and a shovel. Instead, He spoke—and it was so. God said, "Let there be light"—and there was light. "Let us make man"—and man came into existence. When you speak affirmations, you are emulating God, and what could be better than that?

I'd like to propose that you create fifteen affirmations, and that you spend fifteen minutes a day repeating those affirmations to yourself. If you have a willing spouse, partner, or friend, invite them to join you in your affirmation time! These affirmations should represent all the areas of your life in which you would like to see improvement. People often create a dozen affirmations about a specific problem they wish to solve right now, such as overeating. In that case, an individual might write out affirmations like these:

I am a healthy eater.
I eat until I am full and then I stop.
I am able to avoid bingeing.
I am happy with the way my body looks as a result of my healthy eating.
And so on.

A set of affirmations for work might look like this:
I earn $100,000 a year.

I provide great service to my clients, and they love me for it.
I enjoy the support of my boss and my coworkers.
And so on.

Remember that your subconscious mind cannot distinguish between reality and what you say is reality, and that as a result, it will work hard on your behalf to make whatever you say come true. All of the writers who have shaped America's consciousness with regard to prosperity thinking, from Napoleon Hill to Norman Vincent Peale to Catherine Ponder, have taught that affirmations work. Now it's time for you to put these ideas into practice in your life. If you have negative attitudes toward money or those who have money, it's time to identify them and let them go. If you have permitted poverty thinking to create your reality, it's time to stop and shift to prosperity thinking. If you have not yet set goals, it's time to do so. And if you have not created affirmations and begun a process of reciting them daily, for at least fifteen minutes, it's time to do that, as well.

The primary purpose of our mind is to develop faith in God. We then want to use our mind to generate and to receive the ideas that will transform our lives and the lives of those around us. And we want to saturate our minds with prosperity thinking in all its forms. When we are creating healthy bodies for ourselves through diet, exercise, and attitude, and healthy minds, through the ideas we have discussed in this section of the book, we become ready to delve into the most important domain of all—the realm of the spirit. And that's where we go next.

Part III:

Spirit

Chapter 8

Marriage Can Be An Erotic Experience

Judging by the fact that the New Testament speaks of romance and finance as the two most confounding problems mankind faced 2,000 years ago, it sure seems that human nature hasn't changed much over the millennia. We all struggle with relationship issues, and most of us struggle with the concept of money as well. So it was in Jesus' day; so it is in ours.

But it doesn't have to be that way. Life was never meant to be a struggle. The Old Testament patriarchs lived lives of lavish abundance far beyond the imaginings of a Warren Buffett or a Donald Trump. By and large, the marital relationships depicted in the Bible are successful examples of how to love and be loved. Once again, if we take the time to understand God's word and take it to heart, even the thorniest of problems—how to stay happily married, how to keep a healthy perspective about money—fall into place.

In this chapter, I want to talk with you about the concept of Christian marriage and the roles of husband and wife. Contrary to what most popular current commentators will tell you, men and women have distinctly different roles. When men and women live by their Biblically ordained responsibilities, the result is long life, length of days, love, and happy, contented companionship within the marriage structure. There is seemingly little support in today's technology-driven world for something as old-fashioned and seemingly out of date, and even out of touch, as a marriage rooted in scriptural principles. But Jesus knew what He was talking about, as did his disciples, when they provided the now time-tested guidance that has helped countless couples over the centuries find a happy, healthy relationship, a warmth and a love that any of us can attain, provided that we are willing to live by the principles set down in the Bible. Human nature has not changed, and neither has the usefulness and downright common sense inherent in God's word. In this chapter, I'd like to blow the dust off some of those principles, so that you can see how to apply God's word to the most important aspect of your life: your marriage and family.

In Matthew 16:26, the Bible asks, what does a man profit if he gains the world but loses his soul? When we talk of "the world" in this context, we refer to the idea of the financial reward that comes from striving wholeheartedly, and with all of one's energy, toward financial success. "No one can serve two masters. Either he will hate the one and love the other, or he will be devoted to the one and despise the other. You cannot serve both God and Money" (Matthew 6:24). I am not here to criticize the concept of wealth—my reading of scripture makes it abundantly clear to me that God wants us to be wealthy and abundant, mirroring the world that He created for us. The scripture does state in 1 Timothy 1-3 that man should be self-controlled, respectful, and above reproach—not concerned with money. So I'm not here to express contempt for money. I am saying that when we put the material world ahead of our soul and our spiritual development, we are setting ourselves up for terrible loss. Money is important, and indeed the New Testament speaks of the proper place of money in life more than any other topic. But as much as we may love money, it does not have the capacity to love us back! Yes, we can tell ourselves that financial security is paramount, and that it is not just appropriate, but applauded for a man or woman to sublimate all other aspects of his or her personality in favor of worshipping at the altar of the almighty dollar. But the dollar won't love you in sickness and in health. The dollar won't forsake all others for you. We work to make a living, but we love…to make a life.

But how exactly do we love? What does love mean? What is the proper role of a husband and a wife in marriage? How are they to relate to each other? Who's the boss? What's the role of sex? How do you resolve disputes? At what point, if ever, is it appropriate to throw in the towel and say, "I'm outta here!"? And the ultimate question is this: Does the Holy Bible, a document 2,000 years old, really have anything to offer individuals and couples in the Internet age, when old ideas are discarded at a startling rate?

If you've read this far in the book, then of course you know my answer to this. Naturally, the answer is yes. The Bible is sublimely relevant. Sublimely and supremely relevant to the idea of marriage in today's world. Indeed, there is no better guide on the market to successful relationships than the New Testament. The standards are not always easy to live up to, but the rewards are enormous—a blissful, contented married life today, and an entwining of souls with our beloved in the hereafter. Truly, it doesn't get any better than that.

Let's go back to the beginning, the Book of Genesis, to see how the Bible guides us about the relationship between a man and a woman. The first man's name, of course, is Adam, which is derived from the Hebrew word for earth or ground, *adamah*. God brought man into existence last among all the acts of creation during the first six days of the existence of the universe. This demonstrates to us the importance of human beings in the global scheme of things. As the expression goes, man is a little lower than the angels, and as the Bible tells us, he has dominion over all living things. But there was one aspect of his existence that might not have been obvious, perhaps even to God—that sense of cosmic loneliness that Adam felt as he surveyed his world and made ready to rule it, alone.

According to Genesis 2, God cast Adam into a deep sleep and drew from him a rib, from which the first woman, Eve, was fashioned. The English name Eve is derived from the Hebrew name *Chavah*, the Hebrew root of which is "life." And as we are told in Genesis 3:20, "Adam named his wife

Eve, because she would become the mother of all the living." So woman truly is the mother of all life, with the exception of her husband!

Back then, Adam and Eve didn't need eHarmony.com, a church social, or a softball game after work to meet. You could say that dating was a lot easier then, because there were no other choices! Adam was meant for Eve, and Eve was meant for Adam. Obviously, it's easy for we moderns to disparage the Biblical story of creation, believing, as most of us do, more in science than in religion. But there really is no conflict between the scientific explanation for the creation of the universe—the Big Bang theory—and the Biblical story of Ex Nihilo creation, or the creation of something out of nothing, that Genesis presents. But even if you are more comfortable taking the Book of Genesis as metaphor instead of factual truth, the closeness of the relationship between Adam and Eve cannot be denied. That closeness is a metaphor, a Biblical paradigm, for how close a man and woman can be.

Why do men and women marry? Because for us in modern times, as it was for Adam and Eve at the dawn of time, "It is not good for man to be alone." Thus God created Eve as a partner, a companion, and a friend for Adam, so that he would not have to go through his life alone. Interestingly, the Hebrew word *ezer k'negdo*, often translated as "helpmeet" to describe Eve's role in Adam's life, is literally translated as "helper against him." In other words, sometimes a husband and wife help each other, and sometimes they are against each other, or at odds with one another. The Bible understood that from the very beginning. Sometimes we get along, and sometimes we don't.

The Bible is not a guide for angels. It is a guide for people, with all our frailties and foibles, as to how to maximize our time on Earth, by connecting spiritually with God and with others, by learning to love God and others, and by learning to serve God and others. Sometimes we connect with others in a positive way, and sometimes not. The rest of the guidance that the Bible offers with regard to male–female relationships is intended to increase the amount of time that we spend connecting positively and decrease the amount of time that we find ourselves at odds with each other.

The Bible does not expect or extol a frictionless marriage. Indeed, friction, in mechanical terms, is the reason why engines run so well! A little bit of difference is actually a good thing, and the Bible makes clear that men and women were created by different means and for certain purposes. Let's talk about the respective roles that men and women play in marriage.

Much has been made of the Biblical commandment that a man should be the head of the household. What exactly does that mean? Does it mean that the man is always the boss, that he makes all the decisions, and that his word is law as far as his wife is concerned? That was not the Bible's intention, and any married person will tell you that that's not how things work in the real world!

The metaphor that the Bible uses in order to explain the relationship between a man and a woman is the relationship between Jesus and the church. "*Now as the church submits to Christ, so also wives should submit to their husbands in everything. Husbands, love your wives just as Christ loved the church and gave himself up for her...*" (Eph 5:24-26). Jesus is the head of the church, and yet His role is to serve the church, strengthen it, and guide it. So is a man's role in marriage—to serve his wife, to strengthen her, to provide spiritual, emotional, and even financial support to her, so that she can feel secure enough to be her best self.

The "head" of a sports team is its coach. The coach's role is not to boss around his players autocratically, as if he were Moses coming down from the mountain with tablets containing thou shalts and thou shalt nots. Instead, the role of the coach is to make each of his players better, to help each of them live up to their full potential, by sharing the guidance, experience, and wisdom that he has gained throughout his career. So it is in marriage—a man is no more intended by God to dominate his wife than a successful coach should dominate his team. Instead, the guidance and sacrifice that a coach offers his team, that Jesus offered the church, that God offered the world through the sacrifice of His Son, is the model for the husband to follow. Being the head doesn't mean being the boss. All power does not belong to the man, contrary to the misreading of scripture that endures to this day. Rather, a successful marital relationship between the husband and wife requires a delicate balance of power sharing, in which the husband gives his all to his wife, just as Jesus gave His all to His church. The essence of leadership is service.

What, then, is the role of the wife in marriage? Until a generation or two ago, gender roles were clear-cut in society—the man went out in the world to earn his living, just as millennia earlier man went out from the hearth to kill the beast, while the woman developed social ties within the community, kept house, and raised the children. In our crazy world today, the roles of men and women have become jumbled, with the result that it's increasingly unclear what it means to be a man and what it means to be a woman in modern society. I lay only part of the blame for this phenomenon at the feet of the leaders of the feminist movement, who have given us the spectacle of women on the front lines of combat in the Iraq War, separated by thousands of miles from their young children. Is there a more stark and saddening example of the confusion of gender roles that feminism has provoked than this? I can't think of anything more tragic than a young mother maimed or killed in the line of duty, when she could have and should have been home fulfilling her nature and her responsibilities as a mother to her young children. We live in crazy times.

We also live in financially demanding times, and especially in an era of recession and retrenching, it is harder and harder for families to survive on a single income. Here our voracious government is to blame—a second income is necessary not just to "keep up with the Joneses" or to provide the latest in goodies and toys for ourselves and our children, but simply to keep up with the burgeoning tax burden on every family in America. It could be accurately said that the husband goes to work every day to make money to support his family, and the wife is forced to go to work every day to allow the government to live lavishly and spend like a drunken sailor.

Whether it is feminism, economics, or, as I believe, a combination of both factors, it is increasingly hard for a woman who wishes to fulfill her destiny as a stay-at-home wife and mother to do so. And this is one of the great tragedies of modern times.

Is there a Christian solution to this problem? While living within one's means is always a good idea, we begin to see how important the role of the woman is in a marriage. If a man is to be the primary or sole breadwinner, he needs encouragement, warmth, love, kindness, and support from his wife on a daily basis.

To go back to our sports analogy, a coach is responsible for motivating his players not just at every game, but at every practice! A woman's role in a Christian marriage is not to be a giddy, lightheaded cheerleader but instead her husband's greatest supporter, providing him with the encouragement he needs to go out into an increasingly difficult economic landscape and succeed for himself and his family. It has been said that the number one destroyer of career success is lack of emotional support from one's spouse. A woman in a Christian marriage needs to recognize just how important the encouragement, love, and guidance she offers her husband really is. Whether it's a kind word, a gentle expression of the eyes, and a note on the dashboard of the car, or through any other means, her support is the single most important determining factor in his success. A husband may be the primary or sole breadwinner, but without his wife's complete, unconditional, and daily support, he will never maximize his abilities, his gifts, or his income.

So we see the first purpose of marriage is a venue for providing support, a husband for a wife and a wife for a husband, as they each go about their roles. Does the Bible suggest that a woman not be able to work for a living? I don't see anything in the Old or New Testaments that so indicates. There were women judges, prophets, queens, and workers throughout Biblical antiquity. But you would be hard-pressed to find, anywhere in the Bible, an indication that a man is to be a stay-at-home dad, neglecting his financial responsibilities to his family. It is a beautiful thing in today's world that husbands are far more involved with the lives of their children, starting from changing diapers and doing midnight feedings of newborns all the way to helping with college applications. But there's nothing wrong, shameful, or old-fashioned about men and women recognizing and respecting the fact that they have different roles to fulfill in a marriage. In I Peter 3:1-7, these roles are identified:

Wives, in the same way be submissive to your husbands so that, if any of them do not believe the word, they may be won over without words by the behavior of their wives, when they see the purity and reverence of your lives…Husbands, in the same way be considerate as you live with your wives, and treat them with respect as the weaker partner and as heirs with you of the gracious gift of life, so that nothing will hinder your prayers.

If we're going to speak frankly of marriage, we must speak frankly of sex. So let's do just that. God gave sex to human beings, indeed to all species, as a means of procreation, but for human beings, perhaps alone in the animal kingdom, sex can be much more. It is the most divine, complete way to connect with another human being. The Book of Genesis speaks of leaving one's parents and cleaving, or connecting deeply, with one's wife. "For this reason a man will leave his father and mother and be united to his wife, and they will become one flesh" (Genesis 2:24). This is not meant to be understood solely in the realm of relationships, but it is also a signal that a husband and wife are intended by God to enjoy themselves, and to connect deeply—to cleave unto each other—through the miracle and magic of sex.

It's easy to be overwhelmed by the power of sex and either treat it as something to be hated, despised, and feared, and thus to be eliminated from one's daily life, or to take the opposite course and deny that it has any meaning at all. This is the position that modern secular culture takes: considering sex as just another form of entertainment, not much different, and not more meaningful, than, say, going to the movies or going out for a meal. But God's truth steers a middle path through these two obvious fallacies. If we define a man's richness by the strength of his faith, we might say that sex is a poor man's recreation and a rich man's reward. God encouraged Adam and Eve in Genesis 1:28 to "Be fruitful and increase in number; fill the earth and subdue it. Rule over the fish of the sea and the birds of the air and over every living creature that moves on the ground."

When sex takes place within a marriage, it is a holy union, ordained by God no less than marriage itself. It's a beautiful act, in which a couple embraces and says, through their actions, that they are connected and committed. Sex is neither to be feared nor minimized. It matters, it's important, and it is a vital part of marriage. Is sex sinful? Within marriage, the only sin is selfishness. *"Do nothing out of selfish ambition or vain conceit, but in humility consider others better than yourselves"* (Philippians 2:3).

When people use sex as a means of getting their own needs met without regard for the needs or feelings of their partner, disaster is likely to follow. When a man believes that he has the right to expect sex of his wife simply because she is married to him and therefore is responsible for meeting his needs, trouble again will follow, and quickly. Similarly, a wife who regards sex as a means of rewarding her husband for actions taken, words spoken, or money earned is setting the marriage up for disaster. The sexual union in marriage must be freely given and freely obtained. *"The wife's body does not belong to her alone but also to her husband. In the same way, the husband's body does not belong to him alone but also to his wife"* (1 Cor 7:4). The difficulty for a couple busy with work, children, and other responsibilities is finding the time and energy for lovemaking, as practically every married couple can attest! Sex thus becomes the barometer of a marriage. When it's good, the marriage is good. When it is rooted in selfishness or a system where rewarding alternates with withholding, the marriage itself is not likely to be in a good position. So it's essential for couples to steer that middle path between sex as everything and sex as nothing, and instead find that region where sex is the bond, the glue, that creates an everlasting union between two people.

If the only sin is selfishness, then what is selfishness? The Bible considers sex outside of marriage a selfish act. A selfish—and shortsighted—act. Obviously if a society is to endure, families need to have progenitors. If a society is to thrive, the marriage, the home, and the family are the building blocks, because without those essential units in place, there is nothing for a society to build upon. When unmarried people engage in sexual relations, they are going against God's law. That's true whether "everyone" is doing it or whether just a few other members of one's peer group are "doing it." God's law is not relative, and it doesn't change with the times. It was as true 2,000 years ago as it will be 2,000 years from today. The power of sex to bind a couple is misused when it is intended as a form of recreation for unmarried people. That's just the way it is from a Biblical perspective—it is impossible to justify premarital sex from a Biblical perspective.

Extramarital sex, it goes without saying, is even worse, because in that case, we are not simply violating God's law, but violating the trust of the person to whom we made a commitment before God and community on our wedding day. Again, the fact that many people cheat, that it's almost socially acceptable, does not make a difference to the committed Christian. As Gal 5:19-21 tells us:

> *The acts of the sinful nature are obvious: sexual immorality, impurity and debauchery; idolatry and witchcraft; hatred, discord, jealousy, fits of rage, selfish ambition, dissensions, factions and envy; drunkenness, orgies, and the like. I warn you, as I did before, that those who live like this will not inherit the kingdom of God.*

The committed Christian doesn't cheat, period. End of story. Sacred vows are sacred vows. It shouldn't even be necessary to write these words, but we live in an age of such moral relativity that these words really do need to be written, repeated, and indeed, etched on our souls.

If, as I claim, the only sin related to sex is selfishness, within the marriage, prior to marriage, or outside the marriage, then does the Bible recommend or forbid any particular positions or actions? Surprisingly, no. There are certain evangelicals who disapprove of oral sex because this is a practice shared by homosexuals, but this is only one viewpoint within the Christian faith. The Bible itself is silent on the matter. As for masturbation, the story from Genesis of Onan, brother of Er, is often misunderstood. Er died, leaving behind a wife, whom according to Biblical law, his brother Onan was required to marry and support. That's how things worked in Biblical times. Yet Onan did not want to marry his sister-in-law, so at the time that he was expected to solemnize his marriage through intercourse, as was the practice then, the Bible tells us that he *"spilled his seed on the ground."* For this act, he received the death penalty. The act for which he was punished was not masturbation. Rather, it was his refusal to honor his brother's memory by marrying his sister-in-law. This is what invoked God's wrath.

So if no position or approach is specifically excluded by scripture, and if our guideline is that the only sin is selfishness, then pretty much anything within reason is acceptable within a marriage, as long as both parties are comfortable with it, that nothing is being pushed or forced on the other, and neither person is upset by or shamed by a particular practice. In other words, within a Christian marriage, a couple has free rein to express themselves sexually as they see fit, as long as the expression of their sexuality remains within the bounds of the marriage. For *"Whoever commits adultery…destroys his own soul"* (Proverbs 6:32). To avoid such destruction *"The husband should fulfill his marital duty to his wife, and likewise the wife to her husband."* (1 Cor 7:3). That is the Biblical limit to which every Christian must adhere.

If God is a "third partner" within a successful marriage, then perhaps the fourth "person" at the table is Satan. From a psychological standpoint, marriage is the arena in which all our unresolved psychological issues now come to the fore. To put it simply, there's no way you can live with another person without all of your baggage from childhood and young adulthood displaying itself, and usually at the worst times! We all know that we are on our best behavior when we are courting, and that somehow the marriage license is also a license to cease being our best selves with the other person. Behavior that accompanies the sense of "we're married, so now it doesn't matter anymore" ranges from the inconsiderate to the totally unacceptable. In particular the Bible warns against adultery in 1 Corinthians 6:18-20:

> *[F]lee from sexual immorality. All other sins a man commits are outside his body, but he who sins sexually sins against his own body. Do you not know that your body is a temple of the Holy Spirit, who is in you, whom you have received from God? You are not your own; you were bought at a price. Therefore honor God with your body.*

Satan tempts the married individual, not just in terms of seeking a sexual relationship outside the marriage, but also in terms of day-to-day behavior. It's all too easy for people at close quarters, especially when they are tired, to give into the lower aspects of human nature—anger, rage, jealousy, self-pity, manipulation, and the like.

When the Book of Genesis tells us that "sin crouches at the doorway," it's the kitchen doorway, the dining room doorway, and the master bedroom doorway where sin can most easily be found. In a strong Christian marriage, one must overcome Satan's most subtle temptation, which isn't the young woman who works three cubicles away or the good-looking guy at the wife's place of business. Instead, it is the temptation to be our worst self instead of our best self, because we have a sense that "this is what all married couples do" and "I no longer need to be my best self—we're already married."

If you look at the divorce statistics, within and outside of the Christian faith community, it's easy to see that most marriages end. I would be willing to wager that the cause of death for most marriages is not extramarital passion but rather the way married people treat their partners. Our "better angels" want us to be our best selves. As 1 Corinthians 13:4-8 states:

> Love is patient, love is kind. It does not envy, it does not boast, it is not proud. It is not rude, it is not self-seeking, it is not easily angered, and it keeps no record of wrongs. Love does not delight in evil but rejoices with the truth. It always protects, always trusts, always hopes, and always perseveres. Love never fails. But where there are prophecies, they will cease, where there are tongues, they will be stilled; where there is knowledge, it will pass away.

This means that if we as Christians are to emulate the love of Christ for the church, then we must approach our marriages not just from a theoretical standpoint but from a day-to-day, in-the-trenches, in-the-heat-of-the-moment attitude in which we overcome Satan's desire to see us act angrily, or judgmentally, or even cruelly toward the person to whom we committed eternal love, before God, family, and community when we took our marriage vows.

If Satan had only sex to rely on as a tool for destroying marriage, he would have his work cut out for him. Fortunately, he has at his disposal the entire range of bad habits into which all too many married couples slip—anger and rage instead of patience and forbearance, taking people for granted instead of treating people as special, and so on. It is said that idle hands are the devil's playground. In reality, the devil is more interested in us losing our tempers with those we love than losing our souls due to extramarital affairs. If Satan can get couples fighting with each other, the home, the community, and society itself haven't got a chance.

What of divorce? While Jesus tells us in Mark 10:11 *"Anyone who divorces his wife and marries another woman commits adultery against her"* and vice versa, there are certain circumstances in which a couple should not stay together. Physical violence is one such circumstance. If you are the recipient of physical or even strong emotional violence, you must leave quickly. But what about couples who are just going through the typical stresses and strains of marriage, the challenges of raising a family, getting through the financial struggles, coping with in-laws, and the like? God intended marriage to be a molder and shaper of character, and yet, sometimes the challenges within a marriage are too much for a couple to bear. I believe firmly that if more couples based their marriages on the principles of Christian belief as set forth in this chapter, or in practically any book on Christian marriage for that matter, the number of divorces in our society would be radically smaller. But what about cases where a couple really cannot stay together? What is the Bible's position in such sad situations?

The Book of Deuteronomy specifically allows for divorce. If a couple can no longer stay together, a man is permitted to write his wife a decree of divorce, and they are both free to marry others. *"When a man takes a wife and marries her, if then she finds no favor in his eyes because he has found some indecency in her, and he writes her a certificate of divorce and…sends her out of his house"* (Deuteronomy 24:1). Jesus was asked about this law, given the importance that God placed on marriage. And Jesus said, *"Moses wrote that law because your hearts are so hard"* (Mark 10:5). In other words, had individuals been able to soften their positions, perhaps their relationships might have survived and divorce might not have been necessary. So divorce is a Biblically ordained safety valve, permitting marriages that cannot last and perhaps those marriages that should never have been to dissolve. But it is certainly not God's will that couples separate, and certainly not to the degree that they do today.

The Bible understands marriage as a unity of souls not just in this life but for all eternity. This is why the marriage vows repeat the words of Matthew 19:6: *"What God has put together, let no man put asunder."* Therefore divorce has always been an option under God's law, but today it is all too easy a means of ceasing to do the work that marriage—and maturity—require. The problem is that most people who do not figure out what went wrong in their first marriage repeat the same pattern in the next marriage, and the next, and in some cases, even the next one after that. It's not about whom we marry. It's about whom we bring into the marriage—our own personalities. This is why focusing on our own growth is essential in order to have a successful marriage. It's not about finding the right person. It's about being the right person.

How, then, can a Christian find the right person? In today's world, in some ways, it's never been easier, and it's also never been harder. Today there are Christian Websites that allow singles to review each other's backgrounds before meeting, which is certainly an advance over the personals columns of years gone by. The problem is that in our society, couples delay marriage, and children, for increasingly long periods of time, with the result that many individuals are completely burned out on the social scene and have too much of a basis of comparison when it comes to selecting a mate.

A generation or two ago, it was commonplace for a girl to be "pinned" by Christmas of her junior year and engaged or even married by graduation day. Today, the idea of getting married while still in college is almost universally condemned—who could possibly mature enough at that early age to know what he or she wants, or what kind of person he or she wants to be with for all time? I believe we are underestimating the maturity of the modern Christian young man and young woman. If people are rooted in the right ideals, and if their faith is strong, they don't need to wait until their thirties, forties, or fifties to try to find a partner on a Website. As 2 Corinthians 6:14-15 says:

> *Do not be yoked together with unbelievers. For what do righteousness and wickedness have in common? Or what fellowship can light have with darkness? What harmony is there between Christ and Belial? What does a believer have in common with an unbeliever?*

If your belief is strong, if your morality is strong, and if your commitment to doing the right thing is strong, you can be the right person—and therefore find the right person—at any age.

Let's take a couple committed to Christian values and to each other. Is there a "short course" in successful Christian marriage? Yes, and that course begins and ends with the word forgiveness. Indeed, forgiveness implies judging, and judging is God's business, not ours. So the most important thing a couple can have is a good attitude, and a faulty memory. Whatever we pay attention to, grows. The more we pay attention to the faults of our spouse, the harder it is to see anything else other than the spouse's fault. Similarly, if all we see are our spouse's good points, it's hard to get angry—or stay angry—for long. Forgiveness is the key to a successful marriage. *"For if you forgive men their trespasses, your heavenly Father will also forgive you. But if you do not forgive men their trespasses, neither will your Father forgive your trespasses"* (Matthew 6:14-15).

Sometimes people say that marriage is a fifty–fifty proposition—I'll give my fifty, you give your fifty, and that will make a hundred percent. But that's not how it works, as any successful married person will tell you. And it's not a ninety–ten proposition, where each person does ninety percent of the work and expects the other person to do his or her ten percent. In those situations, people commonly say, "Okay, I did my ninety—where's your ten already?" And we're off and running, headed for trouble and eventually the divorce court. And as Zig Ziglar says, "Far more is negotiated in divorce court than on the marriage altar."

No, marriage is not fifty–fifty; nor is it ninety–ten. It is a hundred percent to nothing, meaning that a committed spouse does a hundred percent of what is expected—and that includes love, intimacy, friendship, loyalty, honesty, and all the other virtues that go into being a good person, not just a good spouse. At the same time, the person does not do these things in expectation that the other spouse will be there to perform his ten percent, or fifty percent, or even a hundred percent. We love without expectation and we give without waiting for someone to give to us first. This is the model that Jesus offered the world when He died for our sins—He didn't give fifty percent or ninety percent. He gave a hundred percent. His love for the church was and remains the model for what it means to love and to give another. *"There is no fear in love; instead, perfect love drives out fear"* (1 John 4:18). In Christian marriage, we die not a physical death but an egoic death, as we become willing to put ourselves second and the needs of our spouses first. I said earlier that with regard to sex, the only sin is selfishness. Indeed, that concept could be extended to all of marriage. The only sin is indeed selfishness. If we are selfless, giving ourselves unstintingly, without expectations, without judgment, and with forgiveness, then we can enjoy love in this life with our partner, and with God at our side in the next life as well. It is well said in 2 Timothy 4:7, *"I have fought a good fight, I have finished my course, I have kept the faith."* I wish you and the one you love all the love in the world—God's love.

Chapter 9

Marriage God's Way

God created marriage to be a wonderful and fruitful union between husband and wife. A healthy marriage is a beautiful gift for you and your spouse, as well as a light to the rest of the world. But what if you don't have the marriage that God intended? What can you do to get your marriage back on track and experience all of the many blessings God has in store for you as a couple? In other words, how do you get to God's bottom line for what marriage is meant to be?

It starts with identifying the problems in your marriage. To put God's plan into action, you must first recognize the challenges that you and your spouse are facing. If you've ever been to the doctor, you know that part of getting well involves telling the physician what your symptoms are. You may go into the doctor's office saying, "I'm sick, Doctor. Make me well!" But if you can't describe what's ailing you, your physician's not going to be able to do much. In much the same way, you've got to be honest with God, your spouse, and yourself about where you're struggling. That's the first step to following His plan.

It's no coincidence that one of the main problems married couples face today originated many years ago in the Garden of Eden. God instituted marriage within a *perfect* world, before The Fall (Gen 2:24). But when Adam and Eve committed the original sin, everything changed. What was the basic impulse underlying that sin? Selfishness. Adam and Eve, the very first married couple, gave in to their own selfishness. And ever since, selfishness has plagued the holy union between a man and a woman.

Today, human selfishness continues to undermine the perfect marriage that God intends for all of us. If a husband can say that he puts his self-interest above his wife's, or if a wife can say she puts her own self-interest above her husband's, then there's a problem. Both partners should give 150 percent and not expect anything back. This is easier said than done—we live in an individualistic society where we're told that our own happiness should supersede everything else. But in a Godly marriage, your spouse's happiness is paramount.

Part of making sure your spouse is happy requires spending quality time with each other and paying attention to one another. At its most fundamental, a partnership is about being with the other person. We might think, "Sure, I'm with my spouse all the time." But how much of your day is filled up by other activities? Most people juggle exceedingly hectic and harried schedules. Between getting the kids to school, late afternoon soccer practice, Wednesday night Bible study, preparing meals, long days at the office, and the in-laws coming in for the weekend, it's sometimes difficult just to squeeze in a full conversation with your spouse every day. Instead you end up exchanging a few words and snippets of to-do lists as you pass each other like ships in the night.

Take a moment right now to count up the times in the last week when you have simply allowed yourselves to sit with your spouse, or to have an honest conversation in which you shared your hopes, fears, and dreams with one another. If you're counting on your fingers, you might not even need two hands. How much of the time you could be spending with your spouse is consumed by the insignificant fragments of living day to day? Do you leave enough time to discuss the problems you're facing and the ways you can both grow? And how often do you allow yourselves to truly immerse yourself in your spouse's company, to simply enjoy them for who they are—that person you first fell in love with?

For a marriage to work, both partners need to know that they're needed. Everyone wants to have their opinions heard and valued. Both spouses also need to have a clear understanding that neither would intentionally do anything to upset the other. That doesn't mean that they *won't* do things to upset each other—that's an inevitable risk of being in a close relationship with another human being. But when it happens, each partner must be willing to wholeheartedly ask for forgiveness and move on.

This is especially important when you remember that, in a marriage, two people become one. This is how God meant it to be—marriage is when a man leaves his family and becomes one with his spouse. So when I accept marriage on God's terms, I recognize my wife as my other half. This means that if I do something to hurt her, I'm really hurting myself. And every time I upset my wife or my family, it's not only a form of self-sabotage; it destructive to the joint life we've built together.

You don't have to hit someone to destroy them. Unfortunately, you can hurt your wife or husband without ever touching them. In fact verbal abuse is the most damaging and long-lasting kind of abuse there is. That's why it is so important to be extremely careful in what you say. Choose your words wisely. Always strive to be uplifting and caring, never using your words to destroy your spouse. Build your partner up instead of tearing them down. Choose to speak to one another tenderly, with gentleness and respect. What you give to your spouse in love and compassion will bring the greatest rewards for your marriage.

For just a moment, imagine your marriage as a beautiful palace being constructed. No one ever just throws up a palace within a couple of months and says, "It's done!" The Taj Mahal wasn't completed for well over twenty years, and the Palace of Versailles took fifty. Because palaces are built to last, great time and attention is paid to how they are constructed. As any architect will tell you, the key to building is that every structure must have a firm foundation. Of course palaces can be lovely and lavish—and most are—with turrets and winding staircases and elegant windows that whisper tales of great romance. But it's the structural integrity of the palace that makes it stand strong long after the surrounding shanties and shacks have crumbled to the ground.

The foundation of your marriage is equally vital. Your joint goals and passions—to love one another, to raise a family together, to share God's testimony, to serve—are what keep you focused and committed to one another. Naturally, the most basic element of a strong foundation is the fact that you both believe in God. 2 Corinthians 6:14 says, *"Do not be yoked together with unbelievers. For what do righteousness and wickedness have in common? Or what fellowship can light have with darkness?"* If it feels like you've lost all other semblance of common ground, come back to the fact that you both are believers. Don't downplay the importance of shared faith. You are both committed to living together as heirs of heaven, and to be a helper to one another's souls. Perhaps most important to the issue at hand, you both believe in the holy sanctity of marriage.

God encourages husbands and wives to watch over the hearts and lives of one another, to judge the condition of each other's souls—including strengths, weaknesses, and failings—so that you can apply the most suitable help. Helping your spouse develop can be one of the most fulfilling parts of marriage. Every human life is dotted with its fair share of failings and disappointments. It could be getting fired, losing a loved one, or making mistakes. But it's the hard times that shape us. Look at Job, a man whom God severely tested. Job lost everything, and yet his faith emerged stronger than ever as a result.

When you're married, you have a partner who will stand by your side through the best and the worst of times. Likewise, it is your duty to love your spouse and support him or her all the days of your life. What a gift that is, to be so closely yoked to another person! The fact that you must vigilantly protect the heart and soul of your spouse creates an unspeakable bond. As you grow together, you bear joyful witness to the story of your spouse's life in a way that no one else can.

Now, this doesn't mean you should turn a blind eye to your spouse's faults and problem areas. Helping build up your husband or wife doesn't mean flattering one another out of a foolish, superficial love. We are all sons of Adam and daughters of Eve; hence, we are all sinners. No one is perfect. But instead of nagging or criticizing your spouse, gently urge them to examine themselves. Married couples often find that it's almost impossible to speak to each other about their faults without bitterness and contempt. But addressing your concerns in this manner will only poison the valuable medicine that you could be offering to your spouse. Instead, offers your constructive criticism from a place of love and tenderness.

The flip side is that you, too, must be willing to examine yourself. Don't be the pot calling the kettle black. You must also be willing to accept instruction and constructive criticism from your spouse that enables you to develop into a stronger, wiser, more faithful person. If you refuse to receive and learn from corrections, your spouse will be hesitant to lend a helping hand. No one knows you more intimately than your spouse (at your best *and* your worst), so their instruction is precisely the kind you need. So be open to each other's criticisms. Realize that these are areas where you can grow, and your spouse loves you enough to help you see them. We are often blind to our own weaknesses, and only by having some we know and dearly love gently open our eyes to them can we begin to make significant changes to ourselves and our lives.

Being abundantly honest in your marriage may seem like a given, but some couples don't recognize the importance of honesty. This is another vital part of your palace's foundation—a marriage built on deception and lies (even little white ones) will eventually crack wide open. Rather than concealing the state of your soul or trying to hide your faults, be completely open. Your goal is to be completely known. You are as one flesh, and thus should have one heart. Honesty also means being honest with yourself; being ignorant of your own soul can be just as dangerous as being ignorant of your partner's. Know thyself, so that your spouse may know you, too. Once you know yourself, you'll know better how to treat your husband or wife in the same way that you want to be treated. Remember the Jewish verse that says "A half truth is still a lie".

Knowing how to treat one another is especially important if you have children. Your children are incredibly shrewd observes of how you interact with your spouse—the way you speak and touch each other delivers all kinds of messages about the kind of relationship you have. Even interactions that may seem minor or insignificant—the way you greet each other in the morning, the tone of voice you use when disagreeing about some little thing, the manner in which you share the day's events over dinner—can have a lasting impact on the other people in your household. If you want to raise your children to have happy marriages themselves, you must set a good example in everything you do.

Setting priorities is also pivotal for solving discord in your marriage. Marital harmony is never achieved by focusing on things. No matter what you may see on the television, material possessions don't make people happy. And no matter how much your son is pestering you for a new video game or how often your daughter talks about getting a new phone, things don't make children happy, either. What makes people happy is personal commitment to each other. When you start to privilege your possessions over the people you love, the stuff you own ends up owning you.

Your attitude toward material possessions broaches another common problem area for marriages: money. Very few couples actually make time to discuss and compare their views regarding saving, spending, investing, and the like. And yet these issues end up becoming huge obstacles on the journey toward a Godly marriage. Many couples share joint banking accounts, but they actually have very little knowledge of each other's monetary wishes, tendencies, and bad habits. Why not sit down with your spouse and have a very candid discussion about your views? What financial burdens are you most worried about? How much money have you set aside for the church? Are finances going to be tight for the next few months, but you'll be able to send your son or daughter to college or go on that church mission trip you've been talking about? Just getting an idea of your financial situation—

and how you both feel about it—can be hugely important to improving your relationship.

The key word that should define your approach to money is temperance, temperance, temperance. Galatians 5:22-24 says, *"But the fruit of the Spirit is love, joy, peace, longsuffering, gentleness, goodness, faith, meekness, temperance; against such there is no law. And they that are Christ's have crucified the flesh with the affections and lusts."* When the Apostle Paul lists the Fruits of the Spirit, he closes with temperance, as if temperance is the culmination of the sum total of all these traits. Could the "affections and lusts" to which he's referring possibly have something to do with our lavish and careless use of money? Lusting for wealth seems to be a common affliction. Many of our modern problems stem from the fact that we don't know how to practice temperance when it comes to money. We want that big-screen TV? We buy it. How about that cruise in the Caribbean? Put it on our Visa. The current credit crisis we're experiencing in America speaks volumes about our obsessive tendency to spend without thinking of the consequences. The Bible specifically tells us that money should never own you; unfortunately in today's world, it often does. Thus, to ensure that money doesn't subsume everything else in our lives, we must practice temperance in all things.

God's commandment to practice temperance can mean striking a difficult balance. We are told to be in the world but not of it, and yet our in-world status means that, naturally, worldly things will concern us. As I mentioned earlier, I firmly believe that God intended us to live plentiful and wealthy lives. Take, for example, 1 Corinthians 7:33-34:

> *But a married man is concerned about the affairs of this world—how he can please his wife—and his interests are divided. An unmarried woman or virgin is concerned about the Lord's affairs: Her aim is to be devoted to the Lord in both body and spirit. But a married woman is concerned about the affairs of this world—how she can please her husband.*

In other words, husbands and wives *are* concerned about the affairs of this world—it's only natural. Not surprisingly, money is foremost among them. But by being open with one another about your money problems and concerns, you can alleviate some of the pressure that unspoken worries over finances can cause. You will also strengthen your relationship by building consensus, which creates a unified front against any money-problems that may come your way. And perhaps most importantly, keep Hebrews 13:5 in your hearts and minds: *"Keep your lives free from the love of money and be content with what you have, because God has said, 'Never will I leave you; never will I forsake you.'"* Be soothed by the knowledge that God will care for you, even throughout the most ominous financial woes. Obey God, and you will reap rich rewards.

Spending a lot of money on things can have another negative effect on your family. Let's say you buy a home that's more expensive than you can really afford, or you purchase all new furniture and a backyard pool. As a result, you're plunged into substantial debt, and both husband *and* wife must work fulltime to pay the mortgage and the monthly bills. This can be extremely counter-productive to marital harmony. Suddenly, there are two separate breadwinners in the family. And that's not God's plan!

When so many wives and mothers today are also struggling to maintain a successful career, it can be easy to forget that God intended something very different for us. When a woman takes on the role of the man—making money and providing for the family—it leaves a gaping void in the family unit. If a woman is working long hours away from home, then who will be there to nurture her husband and her children? Who's going to make a priority of cleaning the house, fixing the supper, and doing the laundry? Who will be there when the children get out of school? These roles are all essentially nurturing; they're meant for the caretaker, not the breadwinner. Reversing roles rarely works. And even if it does, it doesn't work as well as the plan God originally put into place. Men who substitute for women are never an equal substitute, nor can women really substitute for men. We each have uniquely special roles that God gave us, and it's when we abide by these roles that we are able to find true peace and fulfillment in our lives.

These are all common problems that afflict married couples today. The first part of solving them is, as we discussed, identifying them. Have an honest discussion with your spouse about what's wrong in your marriage.

Are the two of you operating as one, or are you like two separate people living in the same household? Have you started to conflate roles as husband and wife, and is one of you bearing responsibilities that shouldn't be yours? Are you each giving 150 percent to the other person without expecting anything in return? Or is one of you acting out of self-interest and hurting your wife or husband as a result?

Once you identify the problems in your marriage, you must be committed to solving them, whatever the cost. Sometimes seeking outside support is crucial for working through serious issues, especially when either husband or wife is suffering from a history of trauma or abuse. One solution is marriage counseling, through your church or synagogue or wherever you find the right synergy with your faith. Many churches today have excellent programs with skilled therapists and psychologists who specialize in marital problems. Hypnosis in particular has been extremely effective in restoring marriages to God's glorious design, and hypnosis is especially well suited for dealing with the sexual disharmony that plagues many married couples.

For many people, the word "hypnosis" evokes images of the bizarre and unnatural. But it's not hocus-pocus—it's real, and it does work. Time and again, hypnosis has proven to be a painless and easy way to overcome problems of a sexual nature. Dr. Kenneth Grossman is one of the foremost authorities in the U.S. on hypnosis—I recommend listening to his CDs to get insight on distinctly male and female problems that can be overcome with hypnosis. So often, deeply embedded problems manifest themselves in the sexual relationship we have with our spouse. As we discussed in the prior chapter, sex and money have been the most common marital afflictions since the New Testament Days. But sexual problems are always bigger than money. Sometimes, money becomes a kind of substitute for sexual harmony. My question to husbands who try to solve their marital problems with money and gifts is: Why are you lavishing all these nice presents on your wife? It's not what she wants. After the "thank you" is over, you're still left with the problem. So why not fix the problem instead?

God always intended sex to be a wonderful, vibrant part of your marriage—not a hindrance or problem area. Yet the very fact that there are so many sex therapists in current practice shows that physical intimacy carries with it a lot of contingent issues. Why are there so many hang-ups when it comes to sex? We can answer this question by looking at romantic love from a Biblical perspective. Today, sex has been brutally stripped from the context in which it was intended to bring two people closer: the relationship between a husband and a wife. The practical consequences of sexual immorality are straightforward: people who engage in premarital and extramarital sex must deal with the repercussions of their choices, which can be physical, emotional, spiritual, and mental. They must also suffer God's righteous judgment. "Marriage should be honored by all, and the marriage bed kept pure, for God will judge the adulterer and all the sexually immoral" (Hebrews 13:4).

In today's day and age, particularly with many people having two and three and, God forbid, even more sexual partners, it seems fewer and fewer people go into marriage having saved themselves. Corinthians 6:15-16 says:

> Don't you know that your bodies are part of the body of Christ? Is it right for me to join part of the body of Christ to a prostitute? No, it isn't! Don't you know that a man who does that becomes part of her body? The Scriptures say, 'The two of them will be like one person.'

When two people become like one through sex, they are joined together with the purpose of not separating. Sex is only ever for the marriage partner. This is a big part of why there is so much devastation and heartbreak amongst sexual relationships today—when you share that aspect of yourself with someone and then the relationship doesn't work out, it's literally as if you're tearing yourself in two. The oneness that sex inspires is never meant to end; God intended it to last for a lifetime.

The fact that we have aligned ourselves with the Biblical truth should give us great hope. We must not allow the prevalent sexual immorality of modern society to tarnish sex for those of us who've chosen to live our lives abiding by God's rules and principles. Making love with our spouse is an incredible gift. Sexual union is meant to be the expression and fulfillment of an enduring and unbreakable bond of love. It represents the supreme surrender to another human being because it involves the mutual revelation of each partner's most intimate secret.

As we discussed in the previous chapter, the only sexual sin is selfishness. Withholding yourselves from each other out of spite or malice, or using sex to manipulate your partner, is a sin. *"Do not deprive each other except by mutual consent and for a time, so that you may devote yourselves to prayer,"* says 1 Corinthians 7:5. "Then come together again so that Satan will not tempt you because of your lack of self-control." In other words, if you mutually consent to take a break from sex, that's fine. A temporary reprieve can enable a couple to devote more time to serving and worshipping God. It can also add back an element of excitement and physical energy that many marriages lose; there's nothing like a stint of abstinence to make you long to be with your spouse sexually again. But God commands us that, if you abstain from sex during periods of religious festivals or fasting, you must resume immediately afterwards. God created sex for a reason. Nothing says love better than sex. Nothing says "I care for you" better than sex. While there are other ways to show affection, sex trumps them all.

Sex is meant to be something we delight in, something that brings us great pleasure. When we reveal our most intimate selves sexually to our husband or wife, it's something to rejoice about. The Bible draws a very clear connection between rejoicing and sex. Proverbs 5:18-19 says, *"May your fountain be blessed, and may you rejoice in the wife of your youth. A loving doe, a graceful deer—may her breasts satisfy you always, may you ever be captivated by her love."*

The origin of the word "be" in Greek has two roots: *phyein* and *phynai*. *Phyein* means, "to produce." The natural consequence of being with your husband or wife sexually is that you will have children, thus fulfilling God's commandment to procreate and populate the earth. The other Greek root is *phynai*, meaning, "to be born." Allow yourself to come together with your spouse and be born anew in the love you have for each other. Both of you must cleave to one another, striving for oneness in thinking, purpose, and worship of God. In mutual submission and nurturing, you will experience an invigorating rebirth. The physical oneness that occurs when you make love to one another is the perfect metaphor for the underlining oneness that defines the new life you've built together.

One of the initial yardsticks for marriage is how you felt about each other during your dating or courtship period. The commitment you make before you tied the knot ends up being pretty crucial to how your marriage plays out. Those feelings you felt at the outset can last a lifetime—as long as you continue to prioritize your relationship with your spouse the same way you did when you were courting. When a man finds a woman he wants to spend the rest of his life with, he'll do anything for her. But it's often the case that, once he's married, the pursuit is over. It's the old "thrill of the chase" scenario. After the challenge is won, it's back to business as usual.

But God says this isn't the way it should be. Your wife is the woman you once courted and the woman you still love. She's the same woman you couldn't live without in the early days of being together, and she is now the woman you're married to. Shouldn't you treat her as well now as when you met her? If you do, the relationship will continue to be just as wonderful as it was when it began.

In fact, if you follow God's plan, your marriage will be even *more* wonderful. Why? Because not only will you grow closer to one another; you will continue to grow closer to God as a couple. At the crux of your marriage is God. This should give you great hope in the midst of a world where, statistically speaking, marriages generally fail. Christian marriages are stronger than marriages between nonbelievers because your faith is at the center. You and your spouse both share a fundamental belief in God and his ability to impact your life. Ecclesiastes 4:12 says, *"Though one may be overpowered, two can defend themselves. A cord of three strands is not quickly broken."* In other words, God is the third partner in your marriage, thereby infusing your relationship with a divine and holy strength.

When it comes to sustaining a healthy marriage, Christians are blessed in a number of ways. First of all, we can call on the astonishing power of prayer. When problems arise, a married couple can take them to God. Praying together is a powerful relationship-builder; not only are you growing closer together, but you're growing closer to God. When you are alone, pray for each other and that God will do his work through the heart of your beloved. In addition to being a relationship based on love and commitment between two people, your marriage is also a way to glorify the Creator. God can use a God-centered marriage for His Kingdom—with attendant blessings for your marriage, of course.

Obeying God together will help you grow in your Christian walk. How can you do this? The options are endless. You should be going to church together, worshipping together, signing up for seminars for married couples at your church, joining Bible studies, and even hosting them. Have you thought of opening the doors of your home to other married couples to undertake a study of 1 Corinthians? This is a great way to strengthen your relationship with God and each other while also building a community of fellow believers. The fellowship with other married couples, and the chance to join together in your mutual pursuit of God's wisdom, can enrich spiritual lives of everyone involved.

Some couples shy away from spiritual discussions, worried that their relationship will suffer if they hold differing views. But I encourage couples to speak seriously with each other about these things. If God is at the center of your marriage, then you can only grow closer by talking about Him and His will for your life. Sure, you may disagree about the exact definition of the Elect or the interpretation of a certain passage of scripture, but these are doctrinal differences. At its core, your marriage is built on solid rock: your shared faith in God. Let your discussions be lively and stimulating, but remember to always come back to the truth of what you both believe.

Spiritual discussions can be richly rewarding. There is nothing as exhilarating as discussing your hopes of heaven and eternal life. And you don't have to debate grandiose topics of life and death. Converse regularly about the little things such as the day-to-day trials and tribulations of leading a Christian life. Discuss how your pastor's sermon can be applied to your life. Share spiritual epiphanies with each other. Keep a prayer journal together. All of these things emanate from a natural and shared desire to grow closer to God, which in turn will only bring you closer to one another.

Another component of growing your marriage God's way is to live an exemplary life for His glory. Believing in God is not a stagnant or archaic concept. Faith denotes action and service. Let your marriage bear testimony to all who see it; let it be a way for you to show the world that that you are choosing to glorify the kingdom of God. Don't forget to tithe, and, whenever possible, give money to charity. Love your neighbors, and always be willing to lend a helping hand. If you have kids, encourage them to bring playmates over so that their friends can experience the love of God as it shines through you. Unfortunately, a lot of children today have never had the opportunity to experience God's love, and they certainly don't see it modeled through their parents' relationship. A healthy and vibrant marriage can sometimes be the most effective testimony—it will resonate far more deeply than hollow words or entreaties. So invite your non-Christian friends over to bask in the glow of your Godly marriage. People will long for the trust and intimacy you've established with your spouse, prompting them to ask the question, "How do you do it?"

Don't forget to celebrate the fruits of your belief in God. On a day when your husband has witnessed to a co-worker or your wife has cooked a meal for someone who is ill, rejoice together. Revel in your shared spiritual journey, and herald the pleasures of a mutual faith. Your belief in God further solidifies your belief in your marriage: a fusion of flesh and soul between two people who want to love and serve God.

Your marriage *is* a blessing, to you from God. That doesn't mean that there won't be struggles. There will be moments of darkness and times of trouble, issues you must work through and problems to be faced. It's part of the human condition. But a marriage is so much more than just a human contract. Luke 17:20-21 says:

> *Once, having been asked by the Pharisees when the kingdom of God would come, Jesus replied, "The kingdom of God does not come with your careful observation, nor will people say, 'Here it is,' or 'There it is,' because the kingdom of God is within you.*

The marriage between a man and a woman who love and are devoted to one another provides the perfect example of God's love for us. A marriage is not just an agreement between two people. It's a commitment to serve and love both God and each other. The kingdom of God exists within that holy union; it lives and breathes within your marriage every day of your life. Cherish it, champion it, and defend it with every breath.

Chapter 10

Connecting With God

You have to believe in God.

That's a true statement for every member of practically every religion on Earth. If you don't have God, what's the point of having a religion? This is especially true for us Christians, for whom belief in God is the alpha and omega of our faith.

There's an expression called the "acid test." The acid test refers to whether metal is real gold or not. During the California Gold Rush of the 1850s, miners had a quick and easy way to determine whether metal they had just taken from the earth was gold or valueless, otherwise known as "base." And they simply dipped the metal in acid. Gold did not corrode easily. So the miners would test their metal by dipping it in acid…hence the term "acid test."

Today, God tests our mettle. He tests us by challenging us with problems. Emotional problems, relationship problems, money problems. So the acid test of our faith is this: When God sends us a problem, what do we do? Whom do we call upon? Our own limited abilities, or God's unlimited resources?

The Reverend Norman Vincent Peale used to say that the only people who had no problems...were in the cemeteries! And on those occasions when his life seemed free from problematic challenges, he would turn to the heavens and say, "Hey, God! Don't you trust me anymore?"

In the modern world, where self-reliance is considered a virtue, we tend to handle our problems ourselves...by worrying about them. Instead of taking action, we sit there, or we lie there in bed at three in the morning, turning the problem over and over again in our minds. When we call on ourselves for answers, since we are limited beings, we can only get limited results. But if we have the faith to call on God for answers, we can get unlimited results, because God's power is unlimited.

As the expression goes, if you pray, why worry, and if you worry, why pray? When we're worrying, it's because our faith is not as strong as it needs to be. So instead of viewing problems as interfering with the quality of our lives, instead we need to recognize that problems are blessings in disguise... because they give us opportunities to connect more deeply with God.

Our lives truly are what we make of them. Many of our problems are of our own making. The unfaithful spouse who tears his marriage apart can hardly blame God for the situation that ensues. The businessperson who cheats on her taxes, or lies to clients, sets in motion financial catastrophe. Who's to blame for that, God or the human being?

We can always make a bad situation worse by acting out of our lowest selves. Or we can worry about things that we think we can't control. But if we have faith in God, or read the Bible or whatever spiritual resource is available to you, the answer is abundantly clear.

God says that if you have any problems, call on me. I'll be there for you.

There's not a single religious document in the world, not the Bible, not the Koran, not the writings of the Buddha that says you can pray but God may or may not respond. God always answers prayers. He may not give you the answer you want, but he always provides an answer. If you know that God will answer your prayers and you can trust that fact, then you have a wonderful resource upon which to draw in times of trouble, and in good times as well. God's always there for you. As the expression goes, if you feel distance from God, who moved?

Some people wonder whether God is a better resource than family and friends. In the long run, God is indeed a better resource. Your family and friends will comfort and shelter you. They can give you empathy. They can give you a hot meal, a couch to sleep on, a loving embrace. But can they solve your problems? I do not mean to diminish the value of family and friends, because they are an unparalleled resource. When you think about it, who gave you your family and friends? Who surrounded you with people to support you, people with whom you share a common faith, a common belief? Why, God, of course! God works through people, and God gives us the people who can help us, give us love, understanding, warmth, and perhaps the material things we lack at any given moment. But ultimately, we rely on God, because the source of all our help ultimately is God.

People sometimes think that God doesn't have time for them, that God's too busy, that God's got too many people to take care of, and that it makes no sense for them to reach out to God. Nothing could be further from the truth. God does not work by looking you in the eye and saying, "Here's how to handle your problem." Instead, his blessings, his wisdom, and his peace come to us through other people. A Latin philosopher wrote that God divided man into men, that they might help each other. That's how God works. Your friends and family are there for you, and they are there for God as well—to serve as angels or messengers to give you the love and support you need. But ultimately, the help they provide—and even they themselves—come from God. In short, we are all God's gifts to each other.

Do I believe that God answers prayers? Yes, absolutely. God answers prayers because he promised that he would. In the Bible, he told us that he would answer our prayers. In Hebrew, the word for prayer is closely linked to the word for request. When you pray, you are requesting things from God— health, love, financial success, all good things. And when we request things from God, He has one of three answers for us—yes, no, or maybe later. Is He going to put a note on your pillow that says, "This is my will for you today,

Love, God?" Of course not. That's not how God works. He answers prayers in His way, in His time. Sometimes people don't like the results they get when they pray, because they didn't get the exact answer they were hoping for. So they conclude that God doesn't listen to prayers, or worse, that there is no God. A child might ask his parents for a scoop of ice cream. Is the child always going to get the ice cream? Of course not. Do the parents always love the child? Of course.

When I was a kid growing up in Peoria, Illinois I looked forward to winter and couldn't wait for the snow to fall and the streets to get icy. Snow also reminded me of Christmas and that was my favorite Holiday. As a youngster I went to the Saturday matinees at the Apollo theatre in downtown Peoria. Cowboy movies were the norm and it was usually a double feature with the likes of Lash Larue, Gene Autry, Roy Rogers and The Cisco Kid. At Christmas I sat on Santa's lap and asked for a Red Ryder B B gun. Every year I would ask for it but it wasn't until I was 10 years old that Santa finally granted my wish. During the early years when I received something other than that Red Ryder gun did I ever say "I don't believe in Santa anymore because he doesn't listen to me. He doesn't bring me what I ask for." No, I didn't, not once. He always got me a nice substitute so I knew he loved me. When I was 10 years old I got MY Red Ryder B B gun and I was so excited. It came with a metal target and I took it down stairs in the basement and by Christmas Eve my B B's were gone and the targets were in shreds. Isn't God so much wiser than Santa and don't you believe he knows more about our needs than we do? And I do believe He answers all prayers though they may not be visible in our 'Wants" list but hidden in our "Needs" list. Think about it.

God promised that we would all be part of his family, if we desired that connection to him. If we find ourselves in federal prison, are we still part of God's family? Yes, of course. Perhaps we might have done something that violated not only our own personal ethical norms but the laws of our society. God has not forgotten the prisoner, however. God's love is with the individual behind bars just as much as God is with the person who is sitting in the front row in church. God does not distinguish between His children, and plays no favorites.

That's how things are in this life. It doesn't necessarily mean that we will all have the same place in heaven. There's a judgment day, and we will be judged for what we did with our time here. Our place in heaven depends on what we did with our time and talents on Earth and whether or not we accepted Christ as our Savior. When most people think about judgment day, they think about punishment for sins and rewards for good deeds. But actually, I'd like to take the concept of judgment a step further and ask you this question: What special talents have you been given? Are you making full use of them? Let's say you were born into a family of comfortable means and you received a fine upbringing and a good education. How are you using those gifts? If you are using them to maximize your own abilities so that you can love and serve others, in your family, in your community, and around the world, God will judge you favorably for that. Failing to use the talents we have been given can only be described as a sin. In Latin, the term "sin" comes from archery, and it means, "to miss the mark." The mark that God sets for us, the bull's-eye in this life, is to maximize the use of the talents that we were given. It's not about comparing ourselves to others and thinking that our charitable donations mean nothing because we aren't Bill Gates and we can't give billions to feed the poor. Each of us has the resources to help a poor family or a poor community, get through a day. A week. A month. A year. It's really a question of what we do with the resources we have been given, and those resources include our health, our minds, our upbringings, our education, our careers, and above all, our time.

It's been said that our conscience is in our checkbooks, and there's a great deal of truth to that statement. If you want to see a person's values, take a look at how he spends his money. There's nothing wrong with a nice car, an attractive home, and nice clothes. God wants us to be prosperous, and God wants us to enjoy the best things that life has to offer. But if our priorities are only about material things, then we've completely missed the point. We've missed the mark. We've sinned. How much of our money are we donating to feed the poor? How much are we donating to keep our church in good financial standing? Where do we contribute, and how much? If God judges us strictly by our checkbooks, what would our place in heaven look like? Certainly we cannot buy our way into heaven, but the way we spend our money on Earth is an indication of where we place God in our priorities.

I would like to offer a corollary to the theorem that our conscience is in our checkbooks. You can also find our conscience, or our sense of values, in our day planner. Where do we put our time? A wise man once said that we don't spend time—time spends us. We don't waste time—time wastes us. And ultimately, we don't kill time—time kills us. So the question becomes this: What are we doing with the time available to us? You may remember this verse from your early Sunday school training. Only one life, will soon be past. Only what's done for Christ will last.

Are we plopped down in front of the TV, wasting the precious hours God has given us on mental fast food—satisfying in the moment but of no real nutritional value? Or are we using our time to help those around us? God knows there is a world of people in desperate need of our time and attention. We don't have to move to a far-off land and go on a two-year mission to help others, although there's certainly nothing wrong with that! There's plenty that we can do with our time every day, every week, every month, to make the world a better, more loving, and healthier place. I know people who spend their vacations with their families cleaning beaches, removing trash from them, instead of just lying on them. Or visiting hospital patients, even when they've never met those patients before. It doesn't take much time to make a huge difference in the life of a person or in the life of the world. Let's not judge ourselves solely by how we spend our money. Let's also judge ourselves by how we spend our time, because on judgment day, that is one of the questions that we can count on that God will be reviewing with us. As they say in school, this is going to be on the final!

It stands to reason that those of us who have been given talents and didn't use them, who are given family and friends and abuse relationships instead of doing everything they could to make their relationships great, will not have the same place in heaven as those who use their resources for the common good. So the question then becomes this: How best do you serve God and the people around you? Or to put it more simply, does everyone have a purpose? Remember that the Purpose is in the creation. You were created with special abilities that make it possible for you to fulfill your purpose. Think for a moment about all of God's living creations. Whether it be bugs, birds, snakes, toads, sharks, etc. They were all created with a purpose in a balanced living planet. You are part of that perfect purpose. But you have the ability to know what that purpose is while most of God's creatures just exist day to day without thought to their purpose. They just do what they were created to do. But we are more complex, more versatile and we have the ability to think and change and make choices. He has given us the ability to be more than we ever imagined possible. Knowing that can make life more exciting and creative. Don't ever underestimate your potential or you will be insulting the creator. You will always be less than you are capable of so set the mark high. Trust in God. Can you achieve your dreams and can you serve others in meaningful ways. The answer is absolutely yes. Each of us has a purpose in life. We don't always know what it is, and until our purpose in life becomes clear to us, we prepare for it by becoming the best possible people we can be, by becoming true messengers of God's word. People in Alcoholics Anonymous say that they are often the only copy of the "Big Book," the basic text of AA—that their loved ones, coworkers, and friends might see. So they strive to represent the values of Alcoholics Anonymous in every one of their human interactions. What about us as Christians? Shouldn't we be trying to do the same thing? What if we were the only Christian that those in our immediate world saw each day? Obviously, it's best for a Christian to marry another Christian, but the reality is that when we go into the world, we encounter many people who do not share our faith or our commitment to God. What sort of example of Christianity are we presenting to them? How are we representing God to those who aren't yet believers? Are we walking our talk? Are we living our purpose? Or are we falling short of the behavioral standards to which we know we are obligated to adhere? Whatever your talent might be, whatever your unique purpose in life reveals itself to be, it is your obligation to use those talents for good and not for evil. Sometimes we do fall short of the mark. Some of us, in fact, might be converted, baptized, and saved, truly qualifying for the term "born again". What would happen if two years later, that same person went off on a different tangent and was no longer faithful to their religion? Would they need to start all over?

"Hey, God, I messed up! I want to join again!"

"Will you take me back?" No re-baptism is necessary. You've already made the commitment. God doesn't put any obstacles in your path. Instead, He just says, "Welcome home." Remember the story of the Prodigal son from the Bible? The father welcomed his son home without the need to explain his absence. But, of course, God already knows.

If anything, God expects us to stray. He expects that we will follow our own inclinations until we realize, without the help of divine intervention, that there is a better way, and ultimately, God is waiting for us to surrender to that better way. To paint a word picture, a fisherman can hook a fish, but that doesn't mean that he'll reel that fish in right away. He might give the fish a free line for awhile. Eventually, you'll reel him in when he wears out, when he's exhausted his own resources. I can certainly relate to that image!

God gives us an amazing degree of freedom. It's not preordained that He is controlling our lives. If there were no choice open to us with regard to believing or not believing, what kind of God would He be? A dictatorial God! That's not the God to whom I pray! And I'm sure you feel the same way about your God. Your God, like my God, knows that we can't get credit for choosing if there is no choice. So every day, we opt for God. We make a choice that says that we are putting God's plan for us into action, and we are surrendering our will to His will, and that we are trying to be the best examples we can be of what godly living is all about.

Sometimes people wonder whether God has given any clear direction at all for their lives, other than a vague instruction to do the right thing and be a good person. The answer is that God has absolutely given us clear statements of His expectations. If there are any doubts about what God requests from us, then just look at the Bible. What He tells us is to do the following: "Give me 10 percent of your income. Invest the next 10 percent. And live off the remaining 80 percent (which includes paying taxes). I know a lot of people who follow that biblical formula for financial and life success. They're happy, committed people, and they're going just great, even during the severe economic downturn in which we find ourselves today. They're not concerned about today's headlines. They're prepared for whatever comes, because they have a strategy for living that protects them from the ups and downs of life.

Paradoxically, many other people who do not follow this 10/10/80 plan will tell you that they "live by faith." What they're really saying is this: If I make $1,000, I spend $1,000. And then if I get into difficulties, *at that point* I'll pray and ask for God's help.

To these people I say, you miss the point. God's been helping you for years. You just didn't allocate according to His plan, and now you want Him to make up the difference. Once again, if you are making choices that are not constant with God's will, then don't blame God for the results. If you don't use your resources to get a good education, then you won't have job stability. If you find yourself unemployed, is that God's fault?

If you ask Him to help you find another job, can you count on Him for help in that arena? Absolutely yes. But He's not going to eliminate the trauma and difficulties you're presently going through, because you are reaping the results of the bad choices you made earlier. He'll still answer your prayer, but it won't necessarily be a bed of roses.

I call this approach to life of spending everything one has—or more—instead of tithing to God and saving for the future a crisis lifestyle instead of a Christian lifestyle. Which choice are you making? Whichever choice you make, you will reap the rewards. So you might as well make the choice that benefits you—and the world—the most.

That's God's financial plan for us. In previous chapters in this book, I've talked about God's plan for marriage. Alas, most married people fail to follow that simple plan, and the results speak for themselves. That's how things have been for centuries. And yet can we blame God for a skyrocketing divorce rate? Or should we be looking to ourselves, taking responsibility for our actions, and testing in what ways we are living in appropriate ways, in

God's love for us, and following His plan, and in what ways we are simply following the dictates of our heart. In the Book of Leviticus, God warns us against straying after what our eyes see. It might be another person, or it might be coveting a material good that we really don't need in our lives. Again, how are we using our time, our resources, and our mental abilities? Are we serving God? If so, we'll get great results. If not, we'll get results we don't like, in this world and the next.

As you may have gathered, I am not a fan of many of the results of the feminist revolution in our society. I don't like seeing women in the military, at or near the front lines in the war in Iraq. I don't like seeing an economic system in which more and more women are obligated to work outside the home instead of staying home and raising their children, which many of them would rather do, but for societal pressure that tells them that a stay-at-home mom deserves little respect. Is feminism part of God's plan? No. It's someone's plan, but it's not God's plan. We do have a choice in how we live. We can live in concert with God's expectations for us, and that includes distinguishing between a man's role and a woman's role in the world, in the marriage, and in the home. We do have choices, and we will reap the results, here and hereafter, based on the choices we make.

Is the individual whom we elect to office God's selection or our selection? Who do we complain to if we make a mistake? If God were in total control of everything that happened in the universe, if He were in charge of one hundred percent of the decisions made in our lives and in our country, then we could blame God if we didn't like our elected political leaders and the choices they make. But God's not in control—He shared that control with us by giving us freedom to choose. Our life, therefore, is a choice. Indeed, all the choices that you and I have made have made us the persons we have become today. And the ultimate choice we must make is this question: To whom are we connected? And if we're wise, we recognize the essential wisdom of remaining connected to God.

I'm not suggesting that many of us can live by a black-or-white sense of morality. There are gray areas in which many of us live, and that's where we say, "I'm working on being the kind of person I need to be, and I'm not quite there yet." Are we telling the truth? Are we striving for godliness? Or are we settling for something less, justifying inappropriate or even bad behavior by saying that we're "only human"? Is God only divine? We know that God's priorities are straight. What about ours?

There are lots of people who go to church but don't give their financial resources or time to the church. They think it's not necessary, and they say they might like to donate, but they have no money left over when they pay their bills. They say they've got nothing left.

"I've got to take care of my spouse and my family!" they say. "That's my first priority!"

But that's actually getting things backward. Our first priority as Christians is to take care of God, because God will then take care of us and of our families. By saying that we don't have the money to support the institutions that support our spirituality, we're getting things exactly reversed. It's not what you say—it's not what you do. It's not enough to be a Christian in your heart, which we could call "cardiac Christianity." Instead, it's all about the actions we take given the resources that God has so freely and kindly given to us.

So if you do want to help others, if you do want to use the resources that you've been given, how do you determine what your responsibility should be?

The Bible says love thy neighbor as thyself. But who's your neighbor? Is it Bill next door, whom you lend your lawnmower when he needs it, or maybe twenty bucks to pay the paperboy?

Or is your neighbor a family living in a mud hut half a world away, unable to feed their children because of drought or famine in their land? I have a ministry in the Philippines, which you can learn about at SalisburyFoundation.multiply.com. I go to the Philippines by choice. There, I have the privilege of feeding people whom I have never met and may never see again, with the result that whatever I do has an impact on the lives of these individuals and their children, even if only for a day.

But I have learned over time that to make a difference for a lifetime is more important than for a day. You remember the Biblical advice "Give a man a fish and you feed him for a day. Teach a man to fish and you feed him for a lifetime." So we are expending out thinking and providing tangible items to create income so people can break the dependence on the Government largess. So we recently purchased an electric clothes washer for a woman who was washing clothes by hand to feed her family. Now she has a serious business and can also pay for her daughter's college education as well as feed her family. We recently purchased another larger high capacity washer so she was able to pick up a contract with her local hospital to wash all the linen and blankets, etc. for the next year. To accomplish that, she needed to build another room and hire two more women to iron the sheets. She paid for the room addition herself and we paid for another larger washer as a condition for getting the hospital contract. She was exposed to the hospital contract because her little baby got sick and she took her to the hospital. Over the next few days she asked a simple question, "Who does your laundry?" "Are you happy with the service?" "Who decides who to hire to do your laundry?" She met the hospital administrator and found out the hospital was not happy with the service they were getting. So she asked for the business and the hospital agreed based upon inspecting her facility. Before the hospital comes to inspect one week later she built the ironing room and we bought the equipment. She got the contract for a year. I'll bet that the hospital contract is not the only one she'll get.

I met Anne through my Foundation referral system as she needed 500-peso (about $10.00) to buy milk for her baby. I was in Manila at the time ready to return home but I went to Western Union and sent her money to feed her baby before I went to the airport. She sent me an email when I returned home and the support continued with more thought for financial independence rather than daily assistance.

We've purchased pigs and chickens as well to provide income and growth because that was what people needed. I like to think that we provide the acorn and it will grow into a large strong Oak someday. God provides the resources and we provide the heart for helping. Lest you help the least of my children you do not honor the gifts I've given you.

Again, if you compared the Salisbury Foundation's resources with those of the Gates Foundation, we might look awfully small. But not in God's eyes, and not in the eyes of the individuals, including the children, whose lives we have touched.

In the Old Testament, farmers are commanded not to harvest the corners of their fields, but instead, the produce from the corners of their fields are meant to be left for the poor. Interestingly, the Bible does not specify the size of a "corner." In other words, how much of our resources we share with those less fortunate than ourselves is a decision that we must make. But it stands to reason that the loving God who gave so much to us will reward us for sharing with the least of his children.

If you go someplace and see someone in need, how do you respond? Do you think, I'd like to help but I just can't afford it? Or is your response, I can't afford *not* to help?

What separates me from the poor is God's choice—if He blesses me, it's for a purpose. And He's very clear—my purpose is to bless others. So you shouldn't feel guilty or chagrined or confused that God has blessed you financially. He has done so for a reason—so that you can enjoy your own life and help others enjoy theirs. In the Bible, God is extremely clear about how we are to behave and what we are to do. God wants us to love our neighbor as ourselves, and in so doing, we are putting God first. That's why I say that your "neighbor" isn't just the person in the house next door. It might just be a family in a cardboard shack next to a river in the Philippines. The people in that region are worried about a lot more than losing their job or foreclosure. They're worried literally about where the food will come from for that day. Many families in those poverty-stricken communities will have children because children are a resource—they can go out and beg and get money to eat.

Is that person your neighbor? In God's eyes, absolutely.

You are just as capable of helping the least fortunate, as you are to lend your neighbor a few dollars to meet his need.

One of the saddest things about our world today is the extent to which we waste resources. The money we waste—and I use the term deliberately—on a four-dollar cup of coffee ever day could feed a family every month. I'm not talking about the money you spend on rent, utilities, taxes, or other non-negotiable items. I'm talking about the ways in which we spend our discretionary money. Again, it's all about choice. If God is your best friend, and He does say that all things are possible through Him, and that if you believe in Him you cannot fail, then you have a clear guide to using your resources, financial, emotional, spiritual, and time. If you believe what God says, then why do you keep worrying and avoiding the opportunity and the blessings?

In the beginning of this chapter, we talked about the acid test for gold. Dip gold in acid, and it will not corrode. What about your faith? Can you put it to the acid test? You do, every time you make a choice about allocating the precious resources you have been given. Give first to God, and everything will be added to you. Connect first with God, and the world will be yours. But remember this…sometimes the worst decision is indecision. Now YOU go out and bless others as a personal emissary from God.

Chapter 11

Connecting to God: The 21-Day Plan

So just how do you go out and bless others as an emissary of God? What if you don't think you're an emissary, don't feel ready to share your light with others, or think your faith needs to be strengthened in your personal life first? If you're reading this and telling me that you feel too distant from God to make a difference, then maybe it's time to ask yourself—"Who moved?" In this book I've tried to show what God has in mind for your health, wealth and happiness, but it's up to you to make use of the blessings you've received. And it's up to you to make your faith as strong as it can be.

Fortunately for us, reforming our ways can be easier than it seems. We *are* completely willing to change our habits if we choose to do so! Think about your day-to-day interactions. When you're single and looking for a spouse, you'll probably alter your routines to facilitate getting to know him or her better. Phone calls, meetings, dates and asking questions are all necessary steps in becoming more familiar with someone—and we can do them without thinking twice. Building a relationship with other people may be second nature, but strangely, we may feel like building a relationship with God is too difficult, or we just don't know how. But I've got news for you—

it's easier than it sounds, and it's a lot like making friends. We can't call God up on the phone or meet Him for coffee, but we can take simple steps to alter our day-to-day routines to get to know Him better. And that's what this chapter is about.

We often change our personal habits to become better acquainted with people. When we do this, we're building relationships for our lifetime—relationships meant to make our time on Earth fulfilled and rewarding. But what happens when our time draws near? If you were diagnosed with a serious disease, you would immediately focus on a cure and use your time to get well and extend your life. This would be your new focus. Perhaps if you believed that death was final, you wouldn't make many reforms. You might spend your time trying simply to enjoy the rest of your life. But how many people stop there, and how many people really take a moment to re-evaluate their lives? How many people sit down and ask forgiveness for their sins, and begin to strengthen their relationship with God? We all know that "Death is the Ultimate Reward for Life." But whether that reward is positive or negative is up to us, and our commitment to our faith. What we do during life is important, but it pales in comparison with the time we commit to God. To quote another piece of wisdom, "Only one Life will soon be passed...only what's done for Christ will last." The question is, are you willing to do that footwork to connect with Him? I think you'll agree that more often than not our mortality is a harsh reminder of the importance of secure faith.

I'm sure you've also heard the saying, "Sometimes the worst decision is indecision." Nowhere is that more applicable than to your faith! You may recall the tragedy of Air France Flight 447, which disappeared in the Atlantic Ocean en route from Rio to Paris. Of course I sincerely hope that none of you are ever struck personally with this tragedy. But imagine being on that flight, realizing that you are moments away from certain death. Where do your thoughts go? Who or what are you concerned about? We all remember the words of Christ, reminding us that we cannot enter the Kingdom of Heaven unless we believe in Him and understand that He has already died for our sins. With your last minutes on Earth, would you be scrambling to make peace with God?

As they say in the military, "There's no such thing as an atheist in foxholes." When you're put face to face with death, you immediately recognize your vulnerability. For many people, this means rushing to secure faith in God—maybe because they haven't been as attendant to God lately as they could have been, or maybe they never put faith in Him before at all! But as shocking and scary as these situations are, they aren't meant to secure our faith or *make* us believe. That's our job—not later, but now, so we can fulfill God's mission for us and face the hereafter confident in the strength of our relationship with Him.

Getting closer to God doesn't mean He will answer all your prayers. The question about strengthening your faith, therefore, isn't "What will God give to me?" but "What else can I give in His name?" God knows what's best for us and will provide for us. He will take care of you. But this means that we must be prepared to have our prayers unanswered, even if we know God is watching out for us! Instead of worrying about what else you need in your life, have faith that He will give you what you really need—when you need it. Ultimately, we are trying to equip ourselves to serve God and fulfill the particular mission He has created for us. Becoming the best individuals we can be—by caring for our body, mind and spirit together—is our way of becoming that emissary we're meant to be. This is how we can live every day strong in our faith and bless others as we have been blessed.

It's commonly accepted that we need 21 days to change a habit. In order to bring ourselves closer to God, we must be mindful of bringing Him into our lives each day. This need not be an arduous task. There are quick, simple steps we can take to improve our relationship with God every day. Think about the prayers of Christ—he didn't need fancy language to connect with God, but he was personal and sincere. Although we can take small steps to improve our faith, those steps must be heartfelt. God isn't just a switch that can be "flipped" in our lives. To improve your relationship with Him, you have to put in the time and effort to make Him a part of your life, just as if you were making a new friend—a friend for eternity!

What follows in this book is my own 21-Day Replenishment Plan for connecting with God. Just as in the book, the plan addresses body, mind and spirit in tandem to improve all three at once. I invite you to take this challenge and find new ways to strengthen your faith daily. The items in this plan are simple—most shouldn't take more than 20 minutes a day—and only ask you to make choices to be more mindful of how you go through your day. They're given to you in a list, but remember: to truly make change in your life you need to make them habits, not one-time occurrences! It's not about doing something once, but doing it everyday.

In addition to following the suggestions laid out in the 21-Day Plan, try to consult regularly with your pastor, family and friends for guidance. Set aside time every day for personal prayer connections with God. Think of ways to strengthen your faith that will be most helpful to you, and do them! What you get out of this plan depends on what you put into it.

If you're going to try the 21-Day Plan, make sure to tell someone about it! Being accountable for your work is an important part of your progress, no matter what you do. If you know of a friend who can help guide you in your work, ask them for help. Better yet, perhaps you can follow the plan together and compare results. If you're married, this may be a good time to ask your spouse for the support and constructive criticism he or she is best able to give to help you on your spiritual journey. You may ask your pastor for guidance in your reflections. However you choose to complete this journey, and whom you choose to help you, I hope you'll find it an inviting, effective way to change how you see your life.

So, let's get to it! The 21-Day Replenishment Plan follows here. I wish you all the success in the world on your journey. Before you make your choices for the 21 Day Habit Changing experience, I want you to first go to a Christian Bookstore and buy a picture of Christ to hang in your room. If you are so inclined also purchase a cross to hang on the wall also. These will be a daily reminder of your commitment to change your habits and create a personal relationship with Christ. He is a part of the family of God so make Him a part of your family by putting His picture on the wall. When you pray you can visualize the Christ that you wish to communicate with. He is the Son of God and you should be able to see him with your eyes and feel him in your heart. If there was a picture of God available then I would encourage you to buy that but no sure picture exists. He is represented in everything you see. Take a picture of the Universe and you'll see God.

I am reminded of the story of the little girl in Sunday school who was encouraged to draw a picture of something she learned in Sunday school. Many of the children drew pictures of donkeys, a manager, Mary and Fig Trees etc. This little girl was drawing a picture of God. Her teacher, after asking her what she was drawing, said to her," Well Mary that's nice work but Nobody knows what God looks like." Mary just gave the teacher a big smile and said, "they will now."

Let's proceed now to select those choices most important to your self-improvement and personal relationship to God and prayer. Remember, whatever you choose to do it must be done daily for no less than 21 days and preferably at the same time of day. My suggestion is that you use the morning time when you are awake and are refreshed. Evenings are harder because our bodies are winding down and you may fall asleep while praying.

Choice 1: Take 5 minutes every day to notice the world around you, and to be grateful for it. Notice how magnificent God's Creation is and appreciate it! We take so much for granted and don't stop to look at the details of our surroundings. Sun, moon, stars, oceans, grass, flowers, etc. all marvelous visions of God's creative talent. None of us can conceive of creating anything to compare. If a master painter created a work of art we would honor it and protect it and put the painting in a Museum where it can be safely viewed by the public. Did any painter who ever lived create a picture more beautiful than a real person or a real sunset. The answer is NO. All paintings are nothing more than copies of the Masters creation. So the world become our Museum and we should be the admiring public who can see the Master's works every day and enjoy His immense talent and creativity. We must discipline ourselves to appreciate the beauty we live in. And that should be a part of our daily observance and prayer while we get connected to the Master Creator of the Universe.

Choice 2: Think about your mind for a few minutes. Consider its incredible capacity to learn and strengthen your connection to God, and simply appreciate being given such an amazing gift. Your brain is a funnel for God's messages and answers to prayer. I've heard that we use less than 10% of our brains capacity. Others say less and still others say more. Whatever, it's safe to say that if there is a way to connect to God it is through a mental connection that can only happen if you can "connect" with Him daily through prayer. Does God connect to you through dreams? I think that's possible. Does He connect with you through ideas and creativity? I think He does. When you pray to Him and ask for guidance I think He guides you through thought and through others. If you consider others (including strangers) to be an intrusion on your life comfort and dismiss thoughts as a diversion of your habits then how is God going to communicate with you? You must use and exercise your brain and appreciate its enormous contribution to your life. Think of your life with out a brain! Of course that's impossible because you can't live without one or even think without one.

Choice 3: Philippians 2:3 says, *"Do nothing out of selfish ambition or vain conceit, but in humility consider others better than yourselves."* Think of one new way you can show support to a loved one on a regular basis, and commit to it this week. Add this to your 21-day list and do something nice for someone else every day. If you have time the first day make a list of people who are important to you and honor them with a daily thought and a short gift of time, personal note, gift of flowers or phone call. Remember, do it for 21 days so it becomes a habit.

Choice 4: Meditate on the physical gifts God has given you. Take a moment to be grateful for this godly gift of life and the marvelous complexity of the human body.

Choice 5: Spend some time being honest with yourself about the blocks that keep you from your faith. Are you swamped with responsibilities? Do you feel rushed and tired all the time? Let yourself honor a 5-minute block of time to breathe, relax, and reaffirm that yes: God exists, He cares about us, and He is our Father in Heaven.

Choice 6: Have a conversation with God today before you go to sleep and as soon as you open your eyes from sleep? Maybe you can simply make a habit of spending time to reflect on your day and your plans. Ask for His guidance and at the end of the day thank Him for His guidance. Try to find something simple you can use to "exercise" your mind's ability to strengthen your faith by communicating with Him!

Choice 7: Spend some time today thinking about forgiveness. Are you quick to forgive others? Are there ways you can forgive others more easily in your life? Have you needed to ask forgiveness recently, and how can you request it?

Choice 8: Think of a wish or a goal you've expressed recently. Then ask yourself why you want it, and focus on the real goal of that wish you expressed. Instead of saying, "I want more money because it will make me happy!" say, "I want to make sure happiness is a part of my life!" Write this goal down on a note card and carry it with you so you will see it on a daily basis. Smile and others will return the favor.

Choice 9: Consider different types of exercise at your level of fitness. Whether it be aerobic or anaerobic, from yoga to swimming, think of exercise you might enjoy doing once in a while. My Doctor has said that we need a minimum of 30 minutes of exercise daily to keep our muscles tuned and burn calories. Depending on your age and physical condition, you can do something to maintain your health.

Choice 10: Consider the abundance of God's Creation, the surplus of blessings He has created for our happiness. Think of the ways He wants that in your life. God wants you to be financially secure, to reap the prosperity in the world, and to be *happy* because of it!

Choice 11: For 5 minutes every day, think about one special gift God has given you. Are you blessed with a good job and financial security? Do you have a gift or particular talent? First recognize and thank God for the bounty He has given you—then think of one way you can use it to help others! How can you use the light of God in your life to help the lives of others shine more brightly, too?

Chapter 12

Are We Forgetting How to Communicate?

Sometimes I am critical of different sales and marketing people because I really believe that they've lost the ability to communicate which results in poor service or, more basic, no service at all. I admit that I am biased because I was raised in the mid-west and retained the values that is associated with the older generation raised between the east and west coast. I know there is a different set of values and that fact has been validated by many associates of mine over a period of 40 years. Some of the differences I see are the result of the meaning of "responsibility" vs "irresponsibility". I admit that there is an age bias in addition to a training and upbringing bias.

Let me share some of my pet peeves and see if your age and attitude let's you relate to some of my biases. Let's start with a simple thing like returning phone calls or the new communication entry emails. During my tenure in the securities industry I followed the lead of the most successful brokers and learned how important it is to return ALL calls on the same day that they are received. So if a client or a prospect called me and I was busy with another I was always quick to return calls. The reasons are simple. I didn't know what they wanted until I did return the call. Maybe they wanted to place an order to buy or sell something. Maybe they just had questions that needed to be answered. It is good service to communicate promptly and sometimes to assure the customer that you are there for them. The hardest calls to make, as well as return, are those made after a sudden decline in the market. I remember making calls to clients telling them about losses in their investments and recommending a plan or action. Those were the hard calls but the most necessary. The easy calls were the ones to affirm some profitable transaction so I could gloat a little about my talent to select good investments. But, both good and bad news must be communicated quickly as it is important to clients and demonstrates good service.

You've heard the saying "no news is good news" well I want to tell you it's not true. When you don't make the call then the client thinks that something is wrong and they worry. Answering calls and emails takes little time. Failure to return them creates a lot more work as they have a tendency to build and increase in volume and may create stress as you worry about the calls you don't return. "Maybe they are mad at me, maybe they want to close their account, maybe they want to sue me, maybe it's a creditor, etc. etc." Worry makes it worse. Call immediately and find out the reason for the call. It might even be good news.

Remember how we used to write letters to family, friends and clients. Then you had to wait for days for a response. We used to do mail campaigns with response cards enclosed and wait for the postage paid cards to be returned to see if the mailing was successful. Today we do an email blast to thousands of clients and prospects adding the simple instructions to "click here to register". That's communication in a new and faster way. Despite the new technology my original concern remains the same. The failure to communicate is growing and it is frustrating. You send an email and wait for a response. Someone tells you they will call you back tomorrow and they don't. People make commitments and then forget them. Advertisements for products on radio and T.V. are not truthful and you know it. It seems like dishonest communication is worse than no communication at all.

There are those who will lie to you with no remorse. Students are no longer concerned about the penalty for cheating in school or business. We have to screen those who communicate with us to be sure they are honest. It didn't use to be that way. Or, am I just caught up in imagining the "good old days" as being more honest, more truthful and more dependable. Who can you trust is more than a slogan now. It is a normal defense for doing business. One way to measure honesty is responsiveness. Honest people return phone calls promptly and answer emails quickly. After all, they have nothing to hide and they really want your business and they want to answer all your questions. At least that's how I see it. I guess I am old fashion but I don't like to be put on hold, I want to speak to a real person on the phone and I want to be able to talk to people when I call them or have them return the call the same day so I don't have to carry over my thoughts and questions to another day. How about you?

Are you one of those who have a problem with communication? Can you communicate clearly to your family, your co-workers and friends? As a Christian we have a very clear example of communication by noticing what Jesus did. He was a great communicator and it has been said that the Sermon on the Mount was the greatest motivational presentation of all time. What skills did He have that we can copy. When asked to select the greatest Commandment He said "Love Your Neighbor as Yourself" with the key word "Love". When He spoke his love for his followers and detractors was always clear. Although He did get mad occasionally, as when He was in the temple and chastising the "money changers" He still expressed himself in character. You always knew where He stood on issues. If you didn't understand He spoke in parables so that He could make His point clearly.

He spoke with a singular conviction and firm belief. He knew who he was and what his purpose was. He understood that He was to set an example for others to follow and to "Lead by Example" not just by fancy speeches. If we use Him as an example we should understand that you must speak with sincere love for others, speak clearly and with a singular conviction so no one will be confused by what you say and by what you do. They are singular in purpose and presentation. In dieting they say, "You are what you eat". In life you are "what you say and what you do." Communication can be powerful if done correctly and damaging if misused. History has taught us the power of the spoken word and how it can be used to move nations for both good and bad. If you, your Church or your Company has communication problems you may want to sponsor a seminar on communication. Contact me for details on how this can be accomplished and check on my schedule. The rewards are measurable at every level. I hope to have a positive impact on your life in the near future.

Do you think we are getting better or worse at communication? Let me know your opinion at charlessalisbury1@yahoo.com. Yes, I will respond to your comments. For seminar scheduling call 949-910-6028 or email me.

Afterword

It is all too easy in today's world to neglect one, two or all three of the legs of that three-legged stool in our lives. We may feel like we just don't have the time or energy to commit to improving ourselves, or we may feel like we just aren't capable of achieving everything we feel obligated to do. Life these days can be overwhelming, and social pressures to conform to "the norm" may confront you everywhere. But we have to make time to honor our health, our thoughts and our faith—each and every day—to fulfill the mission that God has ordained for us. If we do, our lives will be richer because our quality of life will improve, and we will know that we are doing just what He wants for us. It can sometimes feel daunting to achieve so much, but in this journey, you are never alone—He will always be there for you, today, tomorrow, and for eternity.

Hopefully, having finished this book and been through the 21-Day Plan, you have become more aware of what God has in mind for your physical and spiritual health, and begun the process of strengthening your faith and connection to Him. Perhaps you have yet to start, but you are thinking of ways to do so. Perhaps you don't feel ready yet. In any case, know that when you feel ready to do God's work, He will be there to support you. I wish you the best of success on your journey of self-transformation, and I hope you feel confident in Jesus' words on the Cross as they apply to you now—to say "It is Finished" to the previous chapter of your life, and to set forward in a newer, better phase of your life. Hopefully the information you've read in this book has taught you how to make your life healthier and more satisfying than before—not just for you, but for your duty as an emissary of God, of course!

I would love to hear from you personally as you continue forward, and I invite you to e-mail me at charlessalisbury1@yahoo.com with any comments, stories or suggestions you have to offer. Your hopes and trials are valuable, and I encourage you to share them with me if you wish. Take care, and God bless.

Message For Muslims

Aired on April 21, 2007
By Chuck Salisbury
Host of "The Incredible Investment Show"

I have a remark about the Muslim faith that I hope will serve a positive purpose. My voice and comments may not be heard by many Muslims but perhaps it will be heard by someone who can do something positive to improve relationships between the Muslim and Christian Faith in the name of world peace.

It's not clear to me that there are Peaceful and Radical Muslims because I can't tell the difference and the Muslim faith is responsible for the lack of distinction. Because I can't tell the radical element vs. the more traditional non-violent members I must err on the side of caution and presume that all Muslims are radical. The reason for this conclusion is simply because the Qur'an preaches violence and the elimination of Christians and Jews. As a Christian, I believe the message is clear…Muslims want to kill me and my family and they want to kill every Christian and Jew without regard for nationality, gender, race or age. To be safe, we are given the choice to abandon our faith and become a Muslim. That will never happen.

As a Christian, I practice the teachings of Christ and believe in forgiveness, love your neighbor and the freedom to choose. I don't see the same choices being given to those in the Muslim faith. No Muslim can ever become an American because they do not subscribe to an important basic tenet of the Constitution which guarantees "Freedom of Religion."

Every Muslim must accept responsibility for my mass condemnation of their faith for the following reason. If any element of the Christian religion and if any clergy member were to form their own militia and teach them to go out and kill innocent women and children in the name of Christ that group would be immediately condemned and totally separated from the Christian community. Every Christian leader would condemn them and their followers and everything would be done to disband the group and change their violent behavior and it would be done **immediately**. The same would happen in the Catholic and Jewish Community. Any teacher, minister, cardinal, bishop or nun would be immediately excommunicated by the Pope and that faith would let the world know that those actions do not represent the Christian, Jewish or Catholic faith.

Where is the condemnation from the Muslim faith when Muslims hi-jack planes and kill 3,000 innocent people, strap bombs to their body and kill thousands of innocent women and children? Have the radical Mullahs been ex-communicated, criticized and removed from their faith by some higher cleric. Does the Muslim faith have a leader who can set standards for the faith and eliminate the Madrasah's where small children are brainwashed from an early age to become followers of Allah and give their lives in order to kill Jews who they refer to as Pigs. If these leaders exist, then where are they and where is the loud condemnation and separation within the Muslim faith? **Failure** to condemn the killing of innocent people in the name of Allah is a form of endorsement.

No major religion in the world honors leaders and teachers of their faith when they teach violence and encourage suicide bombing and the taking of innocent life as a method of gaining admittance into paradise. Take the example of a Mullah in Baghdad called Al Sadr who has a city named after him, Muslim funding for his militia and his mosque and a radical following endorsed by the Muslim faith. The Muslim faith doesn't condemn him; they actually support and encourage him. There are thousands more like him and more added all the time in the name of Allah.

I wish there was a way for me to identify those who are radical from those who are peaceful. Until the Muslim faith identifies themselves as a religion of peace and proves it by decisive action, I will presume that the radical elements truly identify all Muslims and I will do what I can to protect my family and faith from the Muslim faith. Let this word go out and let it multiply in the minds of millions of Christians and Jews who are the targets and are under constant attack. Only one side will win and I know the eventual victor. May HIS return bring peace to all nations.

Written and prepared by:

Chuck Salisbury, Author of *The Incredible Investment Book*
And host of a weekly radio show heard on Saturday mornings

As a shameful example of radical Muslims visit my site dedicated to the victims of the September 1, 2004 attack in Russia. Go to: www.TheChildrenofBeslan.com

ABOUT THE AUTHOR

Nationally renowned real estate authority, Chuck Salisbury has shared his formula for financial freedom with millions of Americans on his syndicated radio program, through speaking engagements, on his web site and his last book entitled The Incredible Investment Book. Today he delights in giving others the opportunity to create their own financial security through the greatest investment in the world, real estate. You can learn more about Salisbury by visiting his company web site www.TenPercentDown.com.

As a lifelong Christian he is also concerned about people's spiritual health and reflects upon his own spiritual journey and realizes that we are losing our moral compass. The more we take our eyes off the influence of Christ's ministry and His specific message for salvation, the more we find ourselves being influenced by secular activities and the relationship experiments of the world. No matter where you travel in the world there is spirituality that always centers around ONE God. He is represented by many prophets and many religions who create their own interpretations of God's word. But as you look around you and focus on the planet you live on you see one world and one central creation. As you look into the Universe and explore those boundaries, you realize the value of any set of rules created by a God who has created everything that we can see and everything we have yet to see.

That advice needs to be taken seriously. With that in mind, Chuck has used the Bible as a resource to provide guidance for those who want to live a Balanced Life…Body, Mind and Spirit. As you explore life beyond your own environment you recognize the Balance that is God's creation. Participate in it, don't fight it.

BUY A SHARE OF THE FUTURE IN YOUR COMMUNITY

These certificates make great holiday, graduation and birthday gifts that can be personalized with the recipient's name. The cost of one S.H.A.R.E. or one square foot is $54.17. The personalized certificate is suitable for framing and will state the number of shares purchased and the amount of each share, as well as the recipient's name. The home that you participate in "building" will last for many years and will continue to grow in value.

Here is a sample SHARE certificate:

YES, I WOULD LIKE TO HELP!

I support the work that Habitat for Humanity does and I want to be part of the excitement! As a donor, I will receive periodic updates on your construction activities but, more importantly, I know my gift will help a family in our community realize the dream of homeownership. **I would like to SHARE in your efforts against substandard housing in my community!** *(Please print below)*

PLEASE SEND ME _____ SHARES at $54.17 EACH = $ $_____

In Honor Of: _____

Occasion: (Circle One)   *HOLIDAY*   *BIRTHDAY*   *ANNIVERSARY*

     OTHER: _____

Address of Recipient: _____

Gift From: _____ *Donor Address:* _____

Donor Email: _____

I AM ENCLOSING A CHECK FOR $ $_____ PAYABLE TO HABITAT FOR HUMANITY <u>OR</u> PLEASE CHARGE MY VISA OR MASTERCARD *(CIRCLE ONE)*

Card Number _____ Expiration Date: _____

Name as it appears on Credit Card _____ Charge Amount $ _____

Signature _____

Billing Address _____

Telephone # Day _____ Eve _____

PLEASE NOTE: Your contribution is tax-deductible to the fullest extent allowed by law.
Habitat for Humanity • P.O. Box 1443 • Newport News, VA 23601 • 757-596-5553
www.HelpHabitatforHumanity.org

Printed in the USA
CPSIA information can be obtained
at www.ICGtesting.com
JSHW082211140824
68134JS00014B/550